CHILDHOOD AND NATURE
DESIGN PRINCIPLES FOR EDUCATORS

CHILDHOOD AND NATURE
DESIGN PRINCIPLES FOR EDUCATORS

DAVID SOBEL

Stenhouse Publishers
Portland, Maine

Stenhouse Publishers
www.stenhouse.com

Copyright © 2008 by David Sobel

Credits:

Chapter 4 is adapted from "Take Back the Afternoon: Preserving the Landscapes of Childhood In Spite of Computers," first published in *Sanctuary* magazine, May/June 1997. Used with permission from *Sanctuary* magazine.

Chapter 5 is adapted from "Mapping McCabe," first published in *Forest Notes* No. 224, winter 1999–2000. Used with permission from article coauthor Susie Spikol and from *Forest Notes*, the quarterly magazine of the Society for the Protection of New Hampshire Forests.

Chapter 6 is adapted from "Authentic Curriculum," first published in *Holistic Education Review*, summer 1994. Used with permission from Psychology Press/Holistic Education Press (https://great-ideas.org).

Chapter 7 is adapted from "Valley Quest," which first appeared in *Orion Afield*, fall 1999. Used with permission from the publisher (www.orionmagazine.com).

Chapter 8 is adapted from "The Sky Above, the Internet Below," first published in *Sanctuary* magazine, January/February 2001. Used with permission from *Sanctuary* magazine.

Chapter 9 is adapted from "Island Play," first published in *Island Journal*, 2007. Used with permission from *Island Journal*.

Chapter 10 is adapted from "Place-Based Teacher Education," first published in *Community Works Journal*, winter 2006, vol. 7. #3. Used with permission from article coauthor Matt Dubel and from *Community Works Journal* (www.communityworksonline.org).

Chapter 11 is adapted from "Global Climate Change Meets Ecophobia." "Global Climate Change Meets Ecophobia" was first published in *Connect* magazine, vol. 21, no. 2 (November/December 2007) and is used here with permission from Synergy Learning International, Inc., Brattleboro, VT (http://www.synergylearning.org).

Library of Congress Cataloging-in-Publication Data

Sobel, David, 1949-
  Childhood and nature : design principles for educators / David Sobel.
    p. cm.
  Includes bibliographical references and index.
  ISBN 978-1-57110-741-1 (alk. paper)
  1. Human ecology--Study and teaching. 2. Outdoor education. 3. Environmental ethics. I. Title.

GF26.S63 2008
304.2071--dc22

                    2007049312

Cover, interior design, and typesetting by Designboy Creative Group
Cover illustration by John Schoenherr. Copyright © 1987 John Schoenherr. Originally published in *Owl Moon*, Philomel Books. Used with permission of the illustrator.

Manufactured in the United States of America on acid-free, recycled paper

20 19 18 17 16 15   10 9 8 7 6 5

Dedication

To my father, **William S. Sobel**, *a truly conscientious parent.
Many of my values and commitments as a parent and educator
are rooted in his care, support, and adventurous spirit.*

Contents

Acknowledgments

I've been following the path to this book for the last twenty years, and there have been many fellow travelers along the way who have provided me with guidance. I apologize in advance if I've overlooked any of my gracious hosts.

Two of these essays were coauthored and I am indebted to the authors for their fine words. Susie Spikol, coauthor of Chapter 5, "Mapping McCabe," and codirector of education at the Harris Center for Conservation Education, is both a lucid and sprightly writer and one of the most child-sensitive environmental educators I know. Matt Dubel, coauthor (actually, 90 percent author) of Chapter 10, " Place-based Education in Guilford, Vermont," similarly is both a fine teacher and writer.

The other codirector of education at the Harris Center, Janet Altobello, is equally attuned to how children connect with nature. Her program designs and work with children have informed my writing continuously.

Each of the design principles has emerged somewhat independently for me, and different people have played a role in helping them come to clarity. My grasp of the significance of nature in the life of the child was inspired, in part, by Louise Chawla. For many years before we met, we had one of those classically wonderful correspondences, mostly handwritten and always intellectually rich. I appreciate my annual research dinners with her.

I learned the importance of *special places* and, more broadly, children's geographical development through the seminal work of Roger Hart. My deeper understanding of the role of special places in the developing psyche of the child was further shaped by Joseph Chilton Pearce. When he picked me up hitchhiking in my early twenties, we had a deeply rich twenty-minute conversation that shaped my intellectual development. Later on, a graduate student essay by Patrice Maynard opened my eyes to the significance of school-yard villages and the role they can play in the life of schools.

I am indebted to Paul Shepard for showing me that much of children's play and development is shaped by our *hunting and gathering* genetic heritage. His writings are a constant source of new ideas for me.

Steve Glazer, the impresario of Valley Questing, has taken the hunting and gathering impulse and turned it into the compelling educational adventure of Questing.

Check out all the quests of Vital Communities in the Upper Valley of New Hampshire and Vermont in his books *Valley Quest I* (2001) and *Valley Quest II* (2004).

I learned the potency of *small worlds* from both Ty Minton and Cia Iselin. Ty taught Marine Ecology, one of the best courses I've ever taken. He used the microcosmic experience of mapping two tide pools in the rocky intertidal zone to serve as the bridge to understanding the macrocosmic principles of ocean ecology. I'm also indebted to both him and his wife, Gael Rockwell, for providing one of my favorite writing haunts on an island off the coast of Maine.

Cia Iselin, inspired by the miniature world of Madurodam in the Netherlands, created the Game of Village, a curriculum for summer camps and schools involving the construction of a 1:25 scale miniature village. The Game of Village remains one of the most potent learning tools I've ever come across. Iselin's vision lives on in many examples in this book.

I learned a lot about *adventures* from my children, Tara Elliott and Elijah Sobel. Canyoneering with Tara and tree skiing with Eli have provided some of the most challenging and fulfilling experiences of my past few years.

For adventures in the classroom, I'm indebted to David Millstone for his great culvert exploration. Jennifer Kramer, whose classroom projects are cited frequently here, deserves special recognition for her commitment to making curriculum come alive through community connections and her deep understanding of children's interests. She makes learning a true adventure.

The term *animal allies* comes from a provocative *Orion* article by Brenda Petersen, which opened my eyes to the powerful relationships between children and animals. Katie Slivovsky and all the education staff at the Brookfield Zoo near Chicago deserve praise for their creation of the Hamill Family Play Zoo—one of the most developmentally appropriate zoo facilities in the country that honors children's relationships with animals.

Maps and paths have been a personal fascination since my father read *My Father's Dragon* to me when I was six. I've pored over hundreds of maps with my good friend Toby Wood, who has been my map-reading companion on countless outings and expeditions in Washington's Olympic Mountains, on Canadian rivers, in Maine's Penobscot Bay fog, and on New Hampshire mountains. Thanks to Casey Murrow, who got me started down this path through being interested in a book about mapmaking with children. Similarly, my appreciation to Julie King, faculty emerita, who helped me cocreate the mapmaking course in which many projects flourished.

I've learned to honor children's *fantasy and imaginations* from working with my colleague Ron Labrusciano in the education department at Antioch New England. His children's literature puppet productions and his lavish impromptu circuses are testimonies to the power of imagination.

I want to extend my appreciation to all my colleagues in the Department of Education at Antioch New England who have supported and inspired my writing for the past ten years. My Integrated Learning colleagues Jane Miller and Judy Coven, along with Ron, have created one of the best graduate teacher-preparation programs in the country because of their commitment to honoring the life of the child in their teaching. In addition, my other colleagues Peter Eppig, Tom Julius, Torin Finser, Arthur Auer, Susan Dreyer Leon, Laura Thomas, and Patty Strohm have often kept the home fires burning while I was off working on this book.

My dear friend Nancy O'Neill read many of these essays in draft form and gave me constructive feedback on how to make them touch the heart most effectively.

Thanks to the Orion Society, and especially Chip Blake, Jennifer Sahn, and Laurie Lane-Zucker for supporting my work and providing an initial vehicle for some of these writings.

And, finally, it's been great to work, once again, with Bill Varner. He was the editor for *Mapmaking with Children*, and he is always sensitive to both the aesthetics of the design and the refinement of the message. He's made this a better book.

CHAPTER 1
REPLACING CONTEMPT WITH LOVE

Kids say the darnedest things, and in those darnedest things are some of the gnarly questions of life. In Richard Louv's (2005) recent book, *Last Child in the Woods*, he quotes one of his children as saying, "What's the relationship between God and Mother Nature—are they married or are they just friends?" I'd like to bring that question down to earth to help clarify the point of this book: What's the relationship between School and Mother Nature? Are they getting divorced or are they committed to working on a long-term relationship?

Let's not even worry about marriage at this point—too tall an order. Instead, let's take it one step at a time. There have been times in the past, say in the early twentieth century during the Nature Study movement, when School and Mother Nature were at least friends. But nowadays, in this No Child Left Behind era, they're quite alienated from each other. To get them back together, School and Mother Nature first need to get to know each other again, then maybe start dating. Eventually they might want to go steady, even consider tying the knot. What might this relationship look like?

I've used these examples before in *Place-Based Education: Connecting Classrooms and Community* (Sobel 2004), but at the risk of being redundant, I'm revisiting them here because they articulate clearly the horns of the dilemma. The divorce option is well articulated in a thought-provoking article entitled "How My Schooling Taught Me Contempt for the Earth" (1996), in which Bill Bigelow describes growing up and going to elementary school in Marin County, north of San Francisco, in the late 1950s.

> *I loved the land. I spent every after-school moment and every weekend or sum-*
> *mer day outside until it got dark. I knew where to dig the best underground forts*
> *and how to avoid the toffee-like clay soil... I knew from long observation at nearby*
> *ponds the exact process of a pollywog's transition into a frog, and the relative speed*
> *of different kinds of snakes: garter vs. gopher vs. western racer... We also had a love/*
> *hate relationship with "development." Almost as another natural habitat, we played*
> *in the houses under construction: hide and seek, climbing and jumping off roofs, and*
> *rafting in basements when they flooded.*
>
> *How did our schooling extend or suppress our naive earth-knowledge and our*
> *love of place? Through silence about the earth and the native people of Tiburon, Bel-*
> *Aire School, perched on the slopes of a steep golden-grassed hill, taught plenty. We*
> *actively learned to not-think about the earth, about that place where we were. We*
> *could have been anywhere—or nowhere. Teachers made no effort to incorporate our*
> *vast, if immature, knowledge of the land into the curriculum. Whether it was in the*
> *study of history, writing, science, arithmetic, reading or art, school erected a Berlin*
> *Wall between academics and the rest of our lives. ...The hills above the school were a*
> *virtual wilderness of grasslands and trees, but in six years, I can't recall a single "field*
> *trip" to the wide-open spaces right on our doorstep. (14–15)*

This is the situation in too many American schools, where children actively learn to "not-think" about the relationships between what goes on inside the school walls and outside in the social and natural communities.

On the other hand, what would it be like if the Berlin Wall came down? What if children were asked to think, rather than not-think, about the earth? In Keene, New Hampshire, the Rachel Marshall Outdoor Learning Laboratory illustrates one such attempt. The initial idea was simple: Develop a three-acre tract of land into a learning laboratory for the five elementary schools, the middle school, and the high school in the city. At the dedication ceremony for a new park that included the Learning Laboratory, Hannah Jacobs (2001), a high school senior, describes how schooling can contribute to the development of a sense of place.

> *The laboratory is truly a little natural world in the midst of bustling Keene. It*
> *is amazing to experience the peace of a forest with cars, horns and sirens all blaring*
> *in the distance. When I was doing research here for my biology project, I stood in awe*
> *as I watched a Cooper's hawk hunting chickadees for a noonday snack. Math classes*

have measured the slope of the land, art and archeology classes at the high school have researched the park's history, and writing classes have sat here to compose pieces with inspiration from nature.

I think the most incredible aspect of the laboratory is its level of community and student involvement. Many students are scared and upset when they see the natural landscape changing around them. We feel like we have no voice in the development of our community, and decisions that are made by the leaders about economic development do affect us significantly and change the character of Keene. The Learning Laboratory actually gave us a chance to make a positive impact and have our voices heard. We were participating in the preservation of a piece of land in our town and deciding how that land would be managed. How refreshing it is to have our suggestions and input listened to, acknowledged and implemented.

How refreshing! Wouldn't it be nice if children came home from school refreshed rather than bored? Instead of the "What-did-you-do-in-school-today?-Nothing" conversation, the response could be, "We followed the stream behind the school down to the Ashuelot River and learned all kinds of river words along the way." Or, "With the slate we got from Mr. Crossman's quarry last fall, we built a new walkway for the school garden. It was hard work, but it came out beautiful." Or maybe, "We went up to Fellsmere Pond and interviewed all the people walking their dogs and sitting on the benches about how the city could make the park better."

All these comments come from children engaged in real projects that connect the core curriculum to real places and real problem-solving in the community. Moreover, these approaches start from inside the child's world, recognizing children's inherent fascinations with nature and people, and then build from these starting points to create sturdy, community-valued knowledge. This is what I'm advocating for—an approach to education that simultaneously honors developing a child's love of the earth and developing a child's academic and social competence.

Let me give you a recent example that weds these two. The eighth-grade social studies curriculum in Vermont calls for students to learn early American history with a focus on colonial America and the Revolutionary War. Some of the standards in the Vermont Frameworks call for:

6.4 Historical Connections: *Students identify major historical eras and analyze periods of transition at various times in their local community, in Vermont, in the United States, and in various locations worldwide, to interpret the influence of the past on the present.*

6.6 Being a Historian: *Students use historical methods to make interpretations concerning history, change, and continuity.*

6.9 Interrelationships: *Students analyze factors and implications associated with historical and contemporary movements and settlements of people and groups at various times in their local community, in Vermont, in the United States, and in various locations worldwide. (Vermont Department of Education 2000)*

Jennifer Kramer, the middle school social studies teacher in Guilford, Vermont, is a master of using local resources to bring the teaching of history alive. She partners with the historical society and town clerk's office. She has a classroom set of the *History of Guilford* as a resource, conducts oral histories, explores local natural resources, and uses cemeteries and census records to engage her students in primary-source investigations. (See Chapter 10 for a description of an autumn's worth of projects in her classroom.) For her unit on colonial Vermont, she knew she wanted to start with having students read the original charter and then develop an understanding of carving a farm and livelihood out of the primeval forested landscape of New England hills and valleys. And she was intrigued with the idea that the charter required that new landowners clear five acres of forested land in five years. Here was the starting point—how could she make this real?

We considered this challenge in a curriculum-planning conversation, and I suggested that we use the children and nature design principles (elaborated in Chapter 3) to identify a childhood fascination that could provide an entrée into the unit of study. We asked: How can children's fascination with *Small Worlds* be used to help students connect personally with the history of Guilford and the history of Vermont? I had used the Small Worlds principle to teach seaside plant communities and ecological design; why not Vermont history? The plan that emerged was to have the students create the five-acre cleared parcels in miniature.

First, Mrs. Kramer gave the students a blank outline map of a Vermont town. Groups of four students had to locate a mill, a meetinghouse, a store, and their own house. Next, a transparency of the rivers, lakes, and streams was layered over their maps, and the students had to decide if this changed their proposed locations. Then a transparency of topography was added, and the students could change their locations one last time. This was an effective way to develop an understanding of the relationship between geographical features and the functions of cultural institutions. Where should the mill be located so that it best serves the needs of the local farmers?

With this basic understanding, students were asked to choose an original Guilford family and one of the original hundred-acre lots and then research early farm life, investigating questions such as:

- What did Vermont farms looks like?

- How were buildings made?

- How did they clear the land?

- What kinds of animals did they have?

- What kinds of jobs had to be done on farms?

Next came the Small World challenge:

Miniature Farms: Clearing the Land and Establishing a Home

On the school's nature trail, find a piece of land that is topographically similar to your family's town lot. Stake out a four-by-six-foot rectangle, representing five acres of your farm, and clear the land and build your family's farm using natural materials from the woods.

Include: a house, a barn, a pasture, an orchard, a water source, cropland, stone walls, and anything else that is historically accurate and reflects classroom reading.

It worked like a charm. In the early spring woods, the eighth graders shed their adolescent cynicism and reentered the world of model trains and dollhouses, yet with clear parameters and content objectives. The vehicle of building a miniature world allowed students to enter into the consciousness of the farmer: Which part of my land gets the most sun and would be best for a garden? Do I place the barn right next to the house? What's the best use of this stony patch adjacent to the outcropping of bedrock? Once the farms were complete, students made sketch maps in the field, which then served as the basis for refined, more formal maps back in the classrooms. The finished products were elegant.

Having settled into their farms, the students were then asked to learn more about their families. Where had they come from? Why did so many children die at an early age? Did my husband really marry my sister after I died? They pursued answers to these questions through visiting local cemeteries, examining burial and census records, reading the town history. This was all assembled into a historical record of the family that then served as the basis for the final challenge:

Newsflash! Rare Discovery in Guilford, Vermont

The Guilford Historical Society reports that a worker has found a dusty trunk in its attic filled with sixty-three diaries of Guilford residents. These diaries describe life in the eighteenth century and include sketches of our town in its early years; never has a treasure like this seen daylight. The president of the historical society reports that "These diaries are really works of art. I've had several calls from museums around the country asking for permission to include these diaries in exhibits."

What does this have to do with YOU? Your job is to create the diaries above. You will use your best historian skills to create the words your Guilford families might have written. Your diaries should be historically accurate, factually rich, and creatively written.

The challenge went on to scaffold specific components the eighth-grade historians had to use in writing the journal. For instance, guidelines for the introductory paragraph read, "Set the scene (and don't forget the date). You're in your special place, and you describe where you are sitting and use all five senses to describe the scene using present tense. What can you see? What sounds do you hear? What smells are present? What do you feel?" Since the students had entered so thoroughly into the land and lives of their eighteenth-century selves, the writing came easily. Excerpts from two journals read:

Asa Rice, 1779

This is where I support my family; this is where I spend my time. I have come to love this barn over the years. God has blessed me with this great structure. The musty smell, the dust from the hay gently floating in the sunlight from the window. I am the only one who can still smell the sweat that rolled off my back during the construction of this building. Memories like that will never leave me. Without this barn, my life would be changed. I have put everything I have into this barn, and it has given even more back...

Sarah Carpenter, May 3, 1798

I love it here in Guilford; its constant joy that every season brings from its flowers and sun in the summer, to its sledding in the breezy, white winters. I love its small and woven-together relationships, both in the families and within the town. I now sit here reflecting on my life and what will come of those who will live on past me and will carry the family's name throughout the history to come…

The writing of all the students was consistently excellent and documented their rich knowledge of life in colonial America. It's also tempting to read this last passage by Sarah Carpenter (an original settler who was an ancestor of the child writing this passage) as both historical fiction and present-day emotion. My hypothesis, supported by conversations with these students, is that this project, and other projects that have connected these students to the Guilford landscape, have led to their love of Guilford and "its constant joy that every season brings."

This is the synthesis of education that creates a love of place and education that builds academic and social competence. And part of the success can be attributed to the teacher's use of the children and nature design principles. The Small Worlds activity served as a transitional metaphor for the students. It was the bridge, the wardrobe to Narnia, that allowed them to enter back into historical times. As you read further, you'll realize that this teacher was using other design principles as well. The early set of mapping activities draws on the Maps and Paths principle; the challenge of writing the discovered journals of old Guilford residents utilizes the Fantasy principle. Woven together, these principles helped create a curriculum that addressed the curriculum standards and went way beyond. Curriculum can lead to sophisticated academic achievement if it grows out of children's fascinations, aims toward substantive content, and aspires to develop ethics of stewardship and community engagement.

This first example is a microcosm of the rest of the book. The next two chapters more deeply describe the foundational value of honoring the child and nature relationship and then portray the role of the children and nature design principles in shaping that relationship. The next six chapters, essays written recently and over the past decade, portray examples of School and Mother Nature getting to know each other. Most of these focus on curriculum in formal educational settings. A few consider the

virtue of natural-world encounters in informal settings where "the play's the thing." The final two chapters connect the design principles to the current challenges in American education today. Do we let ourselves be led down the No Child Left Behind pathway to educational purgatory? Or, instead, do we Just Say No and opt for education that aspires to a healthy balance of head, hearts, and hand?

School can be about getting smarter *and* making the community better *and* protecting nature. Schools can help children love the earth rather than have contempt for the earth. Here's how to get started building this relationship in your school and neighborhood.

CHAPTER 2

"APPARELED IN CELESTIAL LIGHT"
Transcendent Nature Experiences in Childhood

I spend a lot of time these days talking with teachers, foundation directors, environmental educators, and evaluators about how to most effectively shape stewardship behavior. As global climate change looms, it's becoming obvious that we've got to alter our everyday behaviors. The 64-million-dollar question (adjusted for inflation) is, What's the most effective way to educate children who will grow up to behave in environmentally responsible ways? Or, more specifically, what kinds of learning or experience will most likely shape young adults who want to protect the environment, participate on conservation commissions, think about the implications of their consumer decisions, and minimize the environmental footprint of their personal lives and the organizations where they work? There's a surprising dearth of information about exactly how this process works.

Researchers have studied the lives of environmentalists to determine whether there are any similarities in their childhood experiences that might have led to their having strong ecological values and their choice of an environmental career. When Louise Chawla (1998) of Kentucky State University reviewed these studies, she found a striking pattern. Most environmentalists attributed their commitment to a combination of "many hours spent outdoors in a keenly remembered wild or semi-wild place in childhood or adolescence, and an adult who taught respect for nature." Lots of time rambling in neighborhood woods and fields and a parent or teacher who cared about nature were frequently cited as causal forces in the development of their own environmental ethics.

A recent study by Nancy Wells and Kristi Lekies (2006) from Cornell University, entitled "Nature and the Life Course: Pathways from Childhood Nature Experiences to Adult Environmentalism," expands this finding to adults in the general population. The Nature and the Life Course study is one of the first studies of urban residents (your regular

person on the street, not just environmentalists) that looks to link adult attitudes and behaviors with formative childhood experiences. The study is based on interviews with 2,000 adults, ranging in age from eighteen to ninety, chosen randomly from more than one hundred urban areas around the country. Researchers found that

> *Childhood participation in "wild" nature, such as hiking or playing in the woods, camping, and hunting or fishing, as well as participation with "domesticated" nature such as picking flowers or produce, planting trees or seeds, and caring for plants in childhood have a positive relationship to adult environmental values. "Wild nature" participation is also positively associated with environmental behaviors in adulthood.*

What does this mean in everyday language? In his autobiography about growing up in Denver, lepidopterist Robert Michael Pyle describes the urban semi-wild place that inspired him.

> *My own point of intimate contact with the land was a ditch. Growing up on the wrong side of Denver to reach the mountains easily and often, I resorted to the tattered edges of the Great Plains, on the backside of town. There I encountered a century-old irrigation channel known as the High Line Canal. Without a doubt, most of the elements of my life flowed from that canal.*
>
> *From the time I was six, this weedy watercourse had been my sanctuary, play-ground, and sulking walk. It was also my imaginary wilderness, escape hatch, and birthplace as a naturalist ... Over the years, I studied its natural history, explored much of its length, watched its habitats shrink as the suburbs grew up around it, and tried to help save some of its best bits... Even when living in national parks, in exotic lands, in truly rural country side, I've hankered to get back to the old ditch whenever I could ...*
>
> *Even if they don't know "my ditch," most people I speak with seem to have a ditch somewhere—or a creek, meadow, wood lot, or marsh—that they hold in similar regard. These are places of initiation, where the borders between ourselves and other creatures break down, where the earth gets under our nails and a sense of place gets under our skin... It is through close and intimate contact with a particular patch of ground that we learn to respond to the earth, to see that it really matters... Everyone has a ditch, or ought to. For only the ditches—and the fields, the woods, the ravines— can teach us to care enough for the land. (1993)*

To translate this back into academic speak, it was Pyle's childhood "wild nature experiences" in his ditch that led to his adult environmental attitudes and behaviors. The implication is that if we want children to become environmental stewards, then one of the best things we can do is let them play in natural settings.

One problem, of course, is that not every child has a ditch, or even if they do, they're not allowed access to it. Since more than half of the world's children live in urban settings, the availability of ditches, or just urban parklands, is shrinking. Even in rural and suburban settings where patches of woods and ponds are available, parents' concerns about pollution and abduction make these places unavailable. And so the task of providing access to semi-wild places with the tutelage of caring adults often falls to teachers and environmental educators. But as environmental educators seek to professionalize their endeavors and work more closely with schools, they become assimilated into the world of standards, curriculum frameworks, and high-stakes tests. Teachers desiring to take their students outside face the same limitations. As a result, learning about the environment becomes ingesting a sequence of facts and concepts. The underlying assumption is that this knowledge leads to the creation of attitudes that eventually lead to thoughtful environmental behaviors.

Take, for example, this excerpt from a recent set of state standards describing ecology education at different grade levels.

Grades K–4: Identify basic types of habitats (e.g., forests, wetlands, or lakes). Create a short list of plants and animals found in each.

Grades 5–8: Classify local ecosystems (e.g., oak-hickory forest or sedge meadow). Create food webs to show, or describe their function in terms of, the interaction of specific plant and animal species.

Grades 9–12: Identify several plants and animals common to local ecosystems. Describe concepts such as succession, competition, predator/prey relationships and parasitism.

This is a developmentally appropriate sequence of knowledge objectives, but there's an inherent problem. Because these curriculum guidelines are connected to state assessments, the focus often collapses into making sure the students can recite the information. They follow the old Dragnet maxim: "Just the facts, ma'am." As a result, providing the direct experience falls to the wayside. The opportunity to explore the ditch gets replaced by memorizing lists of the plants you might find *if* you actually ever went to the ditch.

Pyle's description shows us where the problem lies. From exploring the ditch, he became interested in natural history and then became an advocate for preservation. Sounds like knowledge to attitudes to behavior. My contention, however, is that the crucial element in his description is, "These are places of initiation, where the borders between ourselves and other creatures break down, where the earth gets under our nails and a sense of place gets under our skin." What gets lost when we focus on facts are the initiation experiences, the moments of transcendence when the borders between the natural world and ourselves break down.

Consider this passage by Dylan Thomas. In his story *Portrait of the Artist as a Young Dog*, he describes two young boys playing along the bushy banks of a stream.

> *Down the thick dingle Jack and I ran shouting, scalping the brambles with our thin stick-hatchets, dancing, hallooing. We skidded to a stop and prowled on the bushy banks of the stream… We crawled and rat-tatted through the bushes, hid, at a whistled signal in the deep grass, and crouched there, waiting for the crack of a twig or the secret breaking of boughs.*
>
> *On my haunches, eager and alone, casting an ebony shadow, with the Gorse-hill jungle swarming, the violent, impossible birds and fishes leaping, hidden under four-stemmed flowers the height of horses, in the early evening in a dingle near Car-marthen, my friend Jack Williams invisibly near me, I felt all my young body like an excited animal surrounding me, the torn knees bent, the bumping heart, the long heat and depth between the legs, the sweat prickling in the hands, the tunnels down to the eardrums, the little balls of dirt between the toes, the eyes in the sockets, the tucked up voice, the blood racing, the memory around and within, flying, jumping, swimming and waiting to pounce. There, playing Indians in the evening, I was aware of myself in the exact middle of a living story, and my body was my adventure and my name. I sprang with excitement and scrambled up through the scratching brambles again. (1940)*

Isn't this a vivid example of "a place of initiation where… a sense of place gets under our skin"? It's these childhood experiences that provide the essential glue, the deep motivational attitude and commitment, the connection to the animals and dirt of the natural world. These primary experiences then fuel the pursuit of knowledge that leads to conservation behavior. John Burroughs (1919) puts it simply when he says, "Knowledge without love will not stick. But if love comes first, knowledge is sure to follow." Too often in schools, we're trying to inject knowledge without providing the experiences that allow love to slowly take root and then flourish.

Which leads me to my controversial hypothesis: *One transcendent experience in nature is worth a thousand nature facts.* Stated in a slightly more positive form, one transcendent experience in the landscape may have the potential for leading to a thousand nature facts. So the question becomes, How do we design family outings, school curriculums, and environmental learning opportunities with an eye toward optimizing the possibility of creating transcendent experiences? Of course, first, we have to get a sense of what these transcendent experiences are and if they really make a difference before we can decide whether they're important enough to pursue.

NATURE MYSTICISM

Writing at the beginning of the nineteenth century, William Wordsworth was one of the first poets to identify the significance of children's nature experiences. In "Intimations of Immortality from Recollections of Early Childhood" (1888), Wordsworth recalls his boyhood wanderings:

❖ ❖ ❖

There was a time when meadow, grove and stream,

The earth, and every common sight,

To me did seem

Appareled in celestial light,

The glory and the freshness of a dream.

❖ ❖ ❖

Wordsworth contended that children perceived nature differently from adults and that this mode of perception was a gift rather than a delusion. Their experiences were transcendent in that the individual often felt connected to or merged with the natural world in some highly compelling fashion.

Following Wordsworth's lead, anthropologist Edith Cobb (1959) reviewed the autobiographies of three hundred European geniuses and found that many of them described similar kinds of experiences in childhood.

> *My position is based upon the fact that the study of the child in nature, culture and society reveals that there is a special period, the little understood, pre pubertal, halcyon, middle age of childhood, approximately from five or six to eleven or twelve, between the strivings of animal infancy and the storms of adolescence—when the natural world is experienced in some highly evocative way, producing in the child a sense of some profound continuity with natural processes...*
>
> *It is principally to this middle-age range in their early life that these writers say they return in memory in order to renew the power and impulse to create at its very source, a source which they describe as the experience of emerging not only into the light of consciousness but into a living sense of a dynamic relationship with the outer world. In these memories the child appears to experience a sense of discontinuity, an awareness of his own unique separateness and identity, and also a continuity, a renewal of relationship with nature as process.*

Cobb's description of these childhood moments of discontinuity and continuity are well expressed in the examples above. Discontinuity is expressed when Dylan Thomas says he is "aware of myself in the exact middle of a living story" and continuity is expressed when he describes the "Gorsehill jungle swarming, the violent, impossible birds and fishes leaping." Pyle's description of his ditch experiences in *The Thunder Tree* capture these same unified polarities.

It turns out, however, that these experiences are not limited to artists, writers, environmentalists, and geniuses. Two similar but unconnected studies document the widespread occurrence of spiritual experiences in nature during childhood. *The Original Vision: A Study of the Religious Experience of Childhood* by Edward Robinson was conducted by the Religious Experience Research Unit at Oxford University in England in 1977. *Visions of Innocence: Spiritual and Inspirational Experiences of Childhood* is a study completed by Edward Hoffman in 1992, a practicing psychologist and university professor who solicited descriptions of childhood experiences from adults in the United States and around the world. Hoffman does not reference Robinson's study, so they appear to be quite independent, though their findings are absolutely resonant.

Robinson's British study was based on adult responses to a published query in newspapers asking people if they had ever "felt that their lives had in any way been affected by some power beyond themselves" (1977). Of 4,000 responses, about 15 percent described childhood experiences and a significant proportion of these occurred in nature. Robinson analyzes these in a chapter entitled "Nature Mysticism." Hoffman's study similarly requested of respondents, "Can you recall any experiences from your childhood—before the age of fourteen—that could be called mystical or intensely spiritual?" (1992). Again, though no mention was made of nature, a significant proportion of the experiences described are nature based.

Both authors state that these are accounts written by adults describing their childhood experiences. Many of the writers suggest that though the childhood experience was monumentally significant, they had no way of describing the experience in childhood. Though swept up in a wave of awe, they had no way to tell their parents what they had felt. Robinson and Hoffman both acknowledge the possibility of the experience being reshaped by years of memory, but the similarity of the descriptions suggests an integrity to the original experience. Let's dip into some of the experiences.

> *When I was about eleven years old, I spent part of a summer holiday in the Wye Valley. Waking up very early one spring morning, before any of the household was about, I left my bed and went to kneel on the window-seat, to look out over the curve which the river took just below the house... The morning sunlight shimmered on the leaves of the trees and on the rippling surface of the river. The scene was very beautiful, and quite suddenly I felt myself on the verge of a great revelation. It was as if I had stumbled unwittingly on a place where I was not expected, and was about to be initiated into some wonderful mystery, something of indescribable significance. Then, just as suddenly, the feeling faded. But for the brief seconds while it lasted, I had known that in some strange way I, the essential "me," was a part of the trees, of the sunshine, and the river, that we all belonged to some great unity. I was left filled with exhilaration and exultation of spirit. This is one of the most memorable experiences of my life, of a quite different quality and greater intensity than the sudden lift of the spirit one may often feel when confronted with beauty in Nature."* (Robinson 1977)

These comments by a forty-year-old woman illustrate Edith Cobb's notion of discontinuity or unique separateness and continuity or oneness with nature. The woman sitting at the window describes "the essential me" (her unique separateness) being unified with the trees, the sunshine, and the river (continuity with nature). I contend that this sense of deep connectedness, of being saturated with nature, yet unique and separate, is one of the core gifts of middle childhood. The sense of continuity provides the foundation for an empathic relationship with the natural world. The sense of separateness provides a sense of agency, of being able to take responsible action for the natural world. The deep bond creates a commitment to lifelong protection. The next question then might be, Are these experiences really specific to childhood? The next

two recollections suggest the discreteness of the developmental window of opportunity. First, from a forty-six-year-old woman:

> *The only aspect in which I think my childhood experience was more vivid than in later life was in my contact with nature. I seemed to have a more direct relationship with flowers, trees and animals, and there are certain particular occasions …in which I was overcome by a great joy as I saw the first irises opening or picked daisies in the dew-covered lawn before breakfast. There seemed to be no barrier between the flowers and myself, and this was a source of unutterable delight. As I grew older, I still had a great love of nature and like to spend holidays in solitary places, particularly in the mountains, but this direct contact seemed to fade, and I was sad about it. I was not quite able to grasp something which was precious.* (Robinson 1977)

And from a thirty-three-year-old German woman who grew up in an urban setting:

> *I can't remember if my parents ever told me that nature is alive or has a certain spirit. But I always felt that nature had a definite soul. In our backyard an old maple tree stood, and I used to climb up it and spend many hours amid its branches. I would hug this old tree, and I always felt that it spoke to me. Its branches and leaves were like arms hugging and touching me, especially on windy days.*
>
> *Not only the trees could speak to me, but also all the plants, streams and even the stones… When I would find an especially beautiful rock on the road, I would take it, feel it, observe it, smell it, taste it and then listen to its voice. Afterward, I would return happily to my parents and relate what the trees or flowers, rocks or brook had told me. They would find this amusing, and were proud of their daughter's imagination…*
>
> *Then school began, and everything changed. Because of my intense involvement with nature, I couldn't relate well to other children who seemed silly and babyish to me. They found me strange and funny. But even harder was the change at home. Now (my parents) denied everything. "What nonsense! The rocks can't talk! Don't let anybody hear this, because they'll think you're crazy."*
>
> *How right my parents were. I found out one day when my classmates saw me talking to a big chestnut tree in front of the schoolyard. Not only did they ridicule me, but they told the teacher, who requested a meeting with my parents the next day…*

My parents recounted the conversation to me and clearly showed how ashamed they were "to have such a crazy child." From that day onward, my magic was systemically ruined or destroyed… So it happened, that I started believing that nature was mute and couldn't speak to me. (Hoffman 1992)

The window of opportunity is both developmental and cultural. Even when a child has a particular disposition toward transcendent experiences, the cultural context tolerates this kind of magical thinking only up through the end of early childhood. It's like imaginary friends—up to about seven they're cute, after seven they become indicative of a child's avoidance of reality.

Both Robinson's and Hoffman's studies are filled with similar descriptions. They become almost boring in their similarity, but that's the interesting part. They seem to reveal a frequent propensity toward transcendent experiences during middle childhood. Certainly, no longitudinal studies have been done to assess whether these people behave in a more ecologically responsible fashion in adulthood than the general population. My speculation, however, is that once you've felt at one with the natural world, it will powerfully compel you to environmental ethics and behavior. Therefore, it follows that if we want to develop environmental values, we should try to optimize the opportunity for transcendent nature experiences in middle childhood.

PLAY AND RELIGIOUS EXPERIENCE

Cultural anthropologist Paul Shepard suggests long-term benefits of these transcendent experiences:

In play, to pretend is to take "as if" as provisionally true: is this an escape from real life, a venture into fantasy, which is more exciting and entertaining than the adult life routine? The answer is yes, it is more exciting; and no, it is not an escape from life. It is a preamble to a special aspect of real life. Like language learning, play is programmed in the human genes and its developmental expression is age-critical. It is essential for the growth of mental life. Apart from its immediate joyful pleasure, it is preparation for a special adult activity: the "as if" of play is the heart of ritual and, eventually, formal religious activity... It is a marvelous example of the wisdom

of the genes that religion functions and is made possible because of the completely instinctive childhood activity, in spite of all its complex intellectual and aesthetic splendor. The ritualizing activity of play is a biological prerequisite to formal religious experience. (1973)

Think about the "as if" in the words of the Catholic sacrament, "Drink this wine, it is the blood of Christ. Eat this wafer, it is his body." The sacrament asks the believer to suspend "reality," to imagine that she is taking in Christ's body. All forms of religion encourage prayer. In Buddhist meditation, the challenge is to step out of the flow of everyday reality, and into a deeper, quieter place. It's like leaving all the noise and arguing in your house and slipping into the private world of your fort. Does your five-year-old daughter's asking her imaginary friend for advice differ from praying to God and asking for help? Does one prepare you for the other? Does the ability to enter into play realities prepare you for the meditative state of prayer?

Further, do we sacrifice a child's capacity to enter a meditative space by not letting him go outside to play in the garden? And, if we keep him inside, does this make it more likely that he'll use alcohol and drugs to find the altered state of consciousness that he didn't find during childhood nature play?

Regardless of how we feel about nature play preparing children for religious experience, I think it's becoming clear that there's a relationship between powerful nature experiences in childhood and adult environmental ethics and behavior. Therefore, it follows that if we want to develop environmental values, we should try to optimize the opportunity for transcendent nature experiences in middle childhood. Tall order? That's where the children and nature design principles come in handy.

CHAPTER 3
CHILDREN AND NATURE
DESIGN PRINCIPLES

DESIGN PRINCIPLES

My overarching goal over the past thirty years has been to look at the relationship between children and nature from the bottom up. This is the opposite of the logic sequence that starts from a problem or a concept in the adult world and then moves downward to impose something on children. The classic example of this top-down mind-set in the past decade of environmental concern has been: The rain forests are disappearing; therefore let's teach children about the horrors of rain-forest destruction so they will act to save them! Instead, I'm more interested in figuring out how to cultivate relationships between children and trees in their own backyards as a precursor to their working to save rain forests as they get older, when they can actually do something about it. Talking to trees and hiding in trees precedes saving trees.

I learn about children-tree relationships through phenomenological observations of children interacting with trees naturalistically. What is it that children actually do with and in trees? Well, they climb them, build forts in them, read in them, hug them, make nests with their leaves, create carnival rides on their branches, play with dolls in their shade, gaze at the sky through their leaves, smell them, become friends with them. Through conducting similar natural-history observations of children in the out-of-doors in all kinds of settings, with children of all ages and in a number of different cultures, certain recurrent patterns emerge. Just as Howard Gardner has identified a set of intelligences in children, I have identified seven play motifs. Regardless of socioeconomic status, ethnicity, or ecosystem, children play in similar ways when they have safe free time in nature.

Now there's really nothing magical about seven. There might actually be five or eleven, but because seven appears to be the set size the mind can easily handle (for instance, traditional seven-digit telephone numbers), I've settled on the lucky number. Spend time at a safe, woodsy playground and you'll find children (1) making forts and special places; (2) playing hunting and gathering games; (3) shaping small worlds; (4) developing friendships with animals; (5) constructing adventures; (6) descending into fantasies; (7) and following paths and figuring out shortcuts. I think there are evolutionary reasons why children do all these things, but regardless of these explanations, it's important to recognize that these activities occur over and over.

To speculate further, it is often in the midst of these kinds of play that the transcendent experiences occur. Look at the experiences described in the previous chapter and you'll see special places in trees, adventures along streams, fantasy conversations, and gathering of flowers. To encourage transcendent experiences or, more simply, just to follow the child's lead in building nature relationships, we can translate these motifs into design principles. In other words, we can use the principles of special places, hunting and gathering, creating small worlds, and the others as design components for family outings, curriculum projects, and environmental field trips.

I'll explore each of the design principles by giving examples of how educators have used these motifs to structure learning experiences for children. In doing so, educators both provide powerful vehicles for curricular knowledge and court the possibility of transcendent experiences. Serendipity rules when the muse will actually show up, but we can invite her.

The design principles are not developmental and, as a result, function at right angles to the developmental stages. The developmental stages of empathy in early childhood, exploration in middle childhood, and personal definition and social responsibility in adolescence provide the warp of the fabric. (These are articulated in *Beyond Ecophobia* [Sobel 1996].) The design principles are the weft of the fabric; they run through all the developmental stages. To take special places as an example, in early childhood, special places are constructed out of couch pillows in the living room and then move to under the porch. In middle childhood, special places are forts out in the woods or up in a tree. In adolescence, the special place might be an electrified clubhouse, or it might become the coffeehouse downtown. Each design principle manifests in a different way in each developmental stage.

I'll spend more time on some design principles, less on others, but they're all equally potent. In *Children's Special Places* (1992) and *Mapmaking with Children* (1998) I explore two of these principles in depth. Also keep in mind that there are no sharp boundaries between one principle and another. They interweave and overlap. In fact, integrating two or three is even more powerful. Here they're separated for ease of presentation.

Principle 1: Adventure

Environmental education needs to be kinesthetic, in the body. Children should stalk, balance, jump, and scamper through the natural world. Activities with a physical challenge component speak directly to children via the mind/body link.

It was a simple transformation. If I suggested to my children that we were going on a walk, they complained. However, if I opened with, "Let's go on an adventure," they were much more recruitable. Walks are for adults. You staidly put one foot in front of the other, you chat about boring things with your friends, you wind up at outlooks and say, "Oh what a beautiful view." Snoresville. Adventures mean you don't know what's going to happen when you start out. You're going to get off the trail, do some sneaking around, surprise someone or get surprised, and you're going to take a few risks. Surprisingly enough, you can cover exactly the same terrain as you would on a walk, but the experience can be completely different.

Taking children into caves, going on blindfold walks, exploring alleyways and dark basements, calling up people you don't know on the telephone—adventures can take lots of forms. I have a preference for the Narnia version, where you start in the everyday and wind up in the exotic. David Millstone (1989), a fifth-grade teacher at the Marion Cross School in Norwich, Vermont, conducted an adventure that integrated mapmaking, writing, vocabulary development, and local history. The accounts of the adventure, published in a school newsletter and excerpted here, illustrate how the true exploratory nature of the event fueled curricular fires.

Predicting Our Path

We were explorers. We set out from the school to solve a mystery. A stream runs by the entrance to the nature area—where does it go? Last week, there were many theories. Fritz drew a map and said it ended in a swampy area in a corner by Route 5 and the interstate. Laura said she wasn't sure where, but she thought it just stopped somewhere. Molly, Lucas and Jake... drew two rough drafts (of a map) before finally agreeing that the stream ended up going into Blood Brook.

I started out thinking it went under Main Street into Blood Brook. But as I drove that way each day to and from school, I couldn't see any likely culverts, and the stream vegetation sloped away to the north. Was there another stream? How did it get past the interstate?

Within the first five minutes, I felt everything going well. "This is great!" someone shouted, and I could hear eager cries and yelling as we moved through the first of many swamps... The stream took a turn north and we followed, twisting and turning with the water, and hesitating only briefly before gingerly entering the culvert—the longest and wettest and darkest culvert I've ever been in. We emerged into the sunlight on the other side of the highway, warm sun and the welcoming face of Ms. Jenks, who opted for the daylight route...

The following two student accounts portray the range of student experience, from poetic to geographic, from Wordsworth to Shackleton.

Shadows, by Molly Witters

Shadows cast on fallen trees covered in soft green moss. It was like a fairy tale, a valley deserted except for the stream running under and over the obstacles of nature...

The hillsides had trees of strange variety from rich green pine trees, to bare and eerie dead trees. There were pools of water where the light hit just right and it looked like a mirror that needed dusting.

We walked along anxiously hoping to see where the stream came to an end. As we approached the spot, five ducks flew off into the piney woods, never to be seen again. I will not go on for the rest of my story would be about mud and noisy highways. I would like to leave my thoughts just where they are, for mud and highways do not come anywhere near to interesting me as much as beauty and imagination do.

The Stream, by Maria McCormick

"We are about to journey into an unknown land," said Mr. Millstone. "No class ever that I know of has been daring enough to do this. If you come to any dangers, monsters or beasts, call for Courtney and she will help you." When we got to the stream we started walking along the side of it. For a short time, we were in the

woods, but then we had to cross a barbed wire fence in a place where it was crushed and we came to a field which I think was the back of the apple orchard. The stream ran through here for a little while until we came to a huge culvert that went under the interstate highway… In the middle there was water dripping down so we had to walk to the side which was hard because it was slippery. (On the bank on the other side), we had our snacks.

Soon we came to a tall fence with a gap at the bottom we had to go under. A little while after that we came to another culvert, smaller than the first one, but still big enough that I could go through it without ducking. This culvert didn't go under any road. Soon after that we came to a very muddy part of the Connecticut River. THIS IS WHERE THE STREAM WENT TO.

Though I have shared only two examples of student work here, you would be amazed at the quality and diversity of the writing and mapmaking. Real adventure provokes real writing. In fact, research indicates that writing that emerges from field explorations of the nearby environment is consistently of higher quality than other writing. This is determined by independent assessments of student writing on the basis of agreed-upon evaluative rubrics.

These student writings illustrate the process of using the design principle as an avenue into inspired learning. At around the ages of nine and ten, children are compelled to push back their geographic horizons, find out what's beyond the next field, make it to the Irish neighborhood beyond Thomas Boulevard. There's an inherent developmental thirst for exploration. By using the adventure and exploration form, the teacher captivates his audience and propels them into deeper learning. In reflecting on this experience, Millstone summarizes.

About Our Hike, by David Millstone

We went for the Great Hike Downstream for many reasons. I was curious about the stream myself, and found in conversations with others that no one really seemed to know where the stream went. The trip expanded our recent emphasis on mapping Norwich neighborhoods. The search would challenge the class's mapmaking skills. Similarly, an adventure into the unknown would stimulate children's creative writing… The experience of following a stream would reinforce a fundamental concept in topographic maps—water flows downhill. The stream flows directly under the new playground, the area we will be surveying for our contour map. I wanted children to experience the thrill of posing a question and working directly to find the answer.

Like any true adventure, what started out as a simple idea grew more complex as we trudged along. We ended up doing things I had not anticipated, and going where I had not planned to go. There was valuable learning for both children and adults in dealing with the unexpected.

Computer simulations like the Oregon Trail have become all the rage in classrooms over the past decade. Students follow the Iditarod, round-the-world sailing expeditions, and the migration of monarchs north, all via the Web. These virtual adventures would be greatly enhanced by real adventure experiences on the schoolgrounds.

To concretize the study of trade along the historic Silk Route, one teacher in Putney, Vermont, had two groups travel from opposite ends of the school forest and meet in the center to trade commodities. By figuring out how long it took them to travel the route in the school forest, the teachers and students figured out how long it would take to travel the thousands of miles on the Silk Route. The real adventure in the backyard provided the basis for understanding the historical adventure in Asia. These kinds of *transitional metaphors* help to bridge the gap from experience to abstraction. Virtual adventure can't hold a candle to kinesthetic adventure.

FANTASY &
IMAGINATION

PRINCIPLE 2:
FANTASY AND IMAGINATION

Young children live in their imaginations. Stories, plays, puppet shows, and dreams are preferred media for early childhood. We need to structure programs like dramatic play; we need to create simulations in which students can live the challenges rather than just study them.

In preparation for a trip to southwestern England about a decade ago, I immersed my ten-year-old son and twelve-year-old daughter in Arthurian legends, Celtic mythology, and Susan Cooper books for a couple of years. One of the trip's goals was to visit lots of variations on castles—ruins, well-preserved medieval residences, military fortifications, baronial homes transformed into country inns. After we arrived at our friend's house in Devon, I proposed the day's agenda.

Daddy: Today we're going to Berry Pomeroy. It's a haunted castle ruins and a historical site. They have a little museum, there's a storytelling program today, and we can have a Devonshire cream tea at the tearoom.

Tara and Eli: Do we have to? (whining with that desultory look on their faces that strikes fear into all parents' hearts)

Daddy: What's the matter? I thought you wanted to go to castles. We've been planning this for years. It should be fantastic.

They looked at each other knowingly, then my son sheepishly turned to me and mumbled,

Eli: Will we have to go on a tour?

Right away, I understood the problem. We do lots of free-form adventuring as a family, but every now and then we do the packaged interpretive experience at a national park or historical site. Most of the time, it drives the kids crazy. Luckily, this day there was no tour. The castle had creepy dungeons and twisty, narrow stone stairways and a storyteller with an old-time ploughman's lunch—a chunk of bread, a slab of cheese, and a raw onion that he ate like an apple—telling local ghost tales. In one of the stories, the key to a cedar chest where the family wealth was hidden played a prominent role. The storyteller shared bits of history and lore, had us creep inside old meat-smoking chambers, led us in singing resonant songs in the chapel, tried to call forth the bats; we played the history of this place for three or four hours.

Months later Eli proudly showed me a rusty key he had found while digging around in an old fireplace. He hadn't told me he found it—sure that I wouldn't let him take it with him. He had actually taken a potential artifact. "I think it might be the key from that story," he speculated. The mystery and history of that misty afternoon were wrapped up in his personal discovery. The moral of this story is that our role as storytellers and world creators precedes our role as imparters of knowledge and cultural heritage.

I ran across a British study a few years ago that further clarified this issue for me. *The Development of Imagination: The Private Worlds of Childhood* by David Cohen and Stephen MacKeith (1991) describes children's private imaginary worlds, which the authors call "paracosms." Paracosms are elaborate fantasy creations—imaginary worlds created by individuals or small groups of children. They tend to emerge around age seven or eight, flourish up through age thirteen or fourteen, and then gradually subside.

One of the originators of the study had a paracosm of his own in childhood and was intrigued to find out whether other adults recalled similar experiences. He solicited accounts via the newspaper (evidently a popular research methodology in England) and lo and behold, he was treated to a wide variety of remembered worlds.

The researchers sifted through the descriptions and decided that in order for a fabrication to be a paracosm, it had to have four key characteristics: "First, children must be able to distinguish between what they have imagined and what is real. Second, interest in the fantasy world must last for months or years...Third, children had to be proud of the world and consistent about it...Lastly, children had to feel that the world mattered to them" (Cohen and MacKeith 1991).

It seems that well-known novelists often created paracosms in childhood. Charlotte and Emily Brontë, authors of *Jane Eyre* and *Wuthering Heights*, respectively, created these worlds with their siblings in their isolated home on the edge of the Yorkshire Moors in the nineteenth century.

> *In June, 1826 their father gave them a set of toy soldiers and this gift sparked into being Verdopolis, the great Glass Town, which later blossomed into the country of Angria. They introduced into it contemporary characters, politicians, soldiers, and writers. They produced a never-ending stream of relevant miniature writings; there were poems and documents, fables and chronicles... Charlotte planned to give up Verdopolis when she went to boarding school and even wrote a poem about its deliberate destruction, but when she came back from school at 16, she soon went back to her imaginary world. In her early 20's, she wrote five little novels about Angria, but these were never published in her lifetime.* (Cohen and MacKeith 1991)

Narnia similarly has its roots in a paracosmic world created by C. S. Lewis and his brother during their childhoods. And lots of nonwriters create them as well. Some worlds are based on toys, some are fairy worlds, others elaborate history, some are reconstructions of existing worlds—like the creation of an optimal boarding school to counterbalance the dreary aspects of a child's current situation. Many of the worlds are independent countries or islands, with a primary focus on geography. One of the subjects of their study, Beryl, created an island world that expanded as she grew between the ages of nine and sixteen.

> *The west coast is rather like Orkney, with high cliffs which tail off to the south where the coastline remains rocky. There are one or two tall stacks like the Old Man of Hoy, palm trees and an abundance of excellent seafood. The south coast was almost tropical, with gorgeous beaches of white sand where turtles came to lay their eggs. On the east coast, a splendidly wide estuary teemed with seabirds and waders… there was a tract called Mohawk Country where there were Indians and herds of wild horses. There were rolling grassy foothills to the north, and beyond them, a phantasy land, peopled by fauns and dryads and the Great God Pan (down in the reeds by the river). I have also seen and stroked a unicorn there.* (Cohen and MacKeith 1991)

Her stories about her explorations and adventures go on and on. As the authors portray, these are not illusory afternoon imaginings, but places in their minds that children return to over and over. And though not all children create lavishly elaborated paracosms, all children create smaller-scale fantasy worlds, and they all get wrapped up in well-crafted stories and opportunities to walk through the wardrobe.

Cohen and MacKeith claim to describe a recurrent childhood truism that we should attend to. Furthermore, I have found that truly inspired teachers (at least all the teachers on my secret Top Ten Greatest Teachers in New England list) create paracosmic worlds in their classrooms through the use of historical simulations, play production, class creation of an evolving story, or involvement in addressing real-life community issues. Families do this through the creation of vernacular family stories with characters and settings that are used over and over for years. (In my family, one of the stories was The Adventures of Princess Quartz and Prince Mica versus the Dragon with the Emerald Chandelier.) Herein lies the design challenge. How can we use elaborated stories and the creation of imagined worlds as a structure for learning experiences for children?

The Forest of Mystery, an annual Halloween event of the Bonneyvale Environmental Education Center in Brattleboro, Vermont, is the perfect manifestation of this concept. Many environmental centers conduct spooky nature programs as fund-raisers during the autumn season, but the Forest of Mystery is a fantastic story in itself that

includes a groundswell of community participation. Each year a new story unfolds. Families arrive at a rambly hill farm with old pastures intergrading into hardwood forests as they rise up the hills. In a weathered barn, around the woodstove, a wizened storyteller lays out the problem and the challenge. Failing crops, strange weather, animals disappearing from the forest, the loss of magic, birds not being able to learn their own songs. As a group of travelers, participants must go into the forest, confront evil, and aid in the village's resurrection.

As you travel the luminaria-strewn path, the story unfolds. Peasants clothed in rags try to unearth meager potatoes from their infertile gardens. Exotic gypsies sing and chant in rhymes, unsure that you have the courage and gumption to confront the forces of darkness. We eavesdrop on the conversation of shrouded spirits as they dine at a formal table set in an oak grove fit for druids. Their crystal goblets clink and their silverware tinkles as their diabolical schemes unfold. Creatures lurk behind trees; sirens attempt to seduce you. But with cunning and courage, we uncage the princess, slay the dragon, and free the villagers in a bonfire ceremony in a high mowing.

The underlying messages of the quest are the fare of the science curriculum standards—wise use of resources, nutrient recycling, concentration of toxins in the food chain, water quality—but the vehicle is story and enchantment. I've been both actor and audience in this experience and each has its own pleasures. As an audience member, I relish the suspension of disbelief, being swept away by eerie lighting that fills the forest with magic and secrets. For just a bit, it feels as mysterious as visiting the graveyard at midnight on Halloween when I was nine. And I appreciate the framing of ecological issues in metaphoric fashion.

In between scenes as a cast member, I covered myself with recently fallen leaves and appreciated having an excuse for being in the woods alone in pitch blackness. In my scene, I enjoyed improvising, figuring out ways to make concepts come alive with that kind of free-form play that happens only in darkened forests.

The Forest of Mystery has many trophic levels of influence. At one level, it remystifies the landscape. "That's one of the most beautiful forests I've ever been in," said my daughter one year. Yes, it's a well-managed forest, but what she's experiencing is the intrigue of the story enhancing her aesthetic appreciation of the place. When children come back here for school-based programs, some of the magic adheres to the place and inspires their learning. At another level, as ecological parable, the stories resonate in children's imaginations, creating visual images for complex concepts. At the community level, it's a social capital–building experience. As cast members, children and adults reacquaint themselves with old friends, forge new relationships, and get to play together through helping to protect the land. As audience, community members get to celebrate Halloween in a ritual that feels more like celebrating the traditional cross-quarter day of All Hallow's Eve (the halfway point between an equinox and solstice) and less like another trip to Kmart.

In schools, teachers construct paracosms often through the creation of classroom plays. Though it's not about children and nature, I heartily recommend David Millstone's (1995) *Elementary Odyssey*, about submerging fifth-grade students in Greek history through a classroom production. Or Steven Levy's (1996) *Starting from Scratch*, in which students enter an empty classroom, devoid of furniture, and literally have to create their own world. Edith Cobb (1959) said that what children want most is "to make a world in which to find a place to discover a self." Our task is to provide the safe place, the tools and materials, and the right stories.

PRINCIPLE 3: ANIMAL ALLIES

Brenda Petersen said, "In our environmental wars, the emphasis has been on saving species, not becoming them" (1993). If we aspire to developmentally appropriate science education, then the first task is to become animals, to understand them from the inside out, before asking children to study them or save them.

Browse through a collection of children's books. Ever notice how frequently animals play a central role? Whether it's *Winnie the Pooh* or *Runaway Bunny* or the Francis books or *Owl Moon*, more often than not either the characters are animals or the people are interacting with animals. It used to be true of cartoons as well, such as Bugs Bunny, Roadrunner, or Rocky and Bullwinkle. No coincidence. Animals play a significant role in the evolution of children's care about the natural world and in their own emotional development. Joseph Chilton Pearce, author of *The Crack in the Cosmic Egg* and *Magical Child*, even contends that a majority of children's dreams are populated with animal characters.

Children feel an inherent empathy with wild and domestic animals. Children's first impulse with some animals is to pick them up, hold them close, take care of them, and become them. Other animals inspire fear and avoidance. Eventually, children may want to hunt such animals, cut them open, and eat them, but that comes a bit later. Just as traditional cultures identified with certain totem animals, children often identify

themselves as a specific animal. Need an icebreaker when trying to get a conversation going with a child? Ask, "What's your favorite animal?"

Paul Shepard suggests that these strong feelings toward animals in early and middle childhood are indicative of our evolutionary heritage. More than 95 percent of our evolution as a species occurred during the preagrarian period when our ancestors were hunters and gatherers. These traditional cultures depended on men's knowledge of animals and hunting skills and women's knowledge of plants and gathering skills. As a result, many of the patterns of our early learning are rooted in learning about animals and plants, what Shepard refers to as "loading the ark of the mind." Early relationships with flora and fauna are an integral part of feeling bonded to the matrix of the earth.

> *A decade, from the beginnings of speech to the onset of puberty, is all we have to load the ark. The zoology of this period must be unequivocal, without recondite allusions. Poetry and song must mean what they say; games must be nothing but play, as unmistakable as a cat chasing a ball. It is right for the child to mimic fox and goose in a game of pretended capture, or speak the lines of the little pig or Chicken Little. By identifying with a number of animals in turn, the child discovers a common ground with other beings despite external differences between himself and them. Anthropomorphism at this stage is essential.... By pretending that animals speak to one another, he imposed on them a pseudo-humanity which, although illusory, is the glue of real kinship.* (1983)

This notion of constructive anthropomorphizing flies in the face of the prevailing scientific mind-set that anthropomorphizing is unhealthy because it imposes a human face on animals. Rather, I agree with Shepard that projecting feelings and human characteristics onto animals facilitates relationships. It makes animals and people part of one larger family, with kinship relationships and rules for sharing and caretaking that weave the clans together. This tendency to anthropomorphize probably grows out of that merged experience of subjective and objective worlds in early childhood, an inability to differentiate between what happens to you and what happens to someone or something else. But rather than consider this as immature or undeveloped, we can consider it advantageous as an opportunity to create empathy, a feeling for other creatures that can develop into a willingness to care for other creatures.

Stephen Kellert, one of the editors of *The Biophilia Hypothesis*, conducted developmental research on urban and rural children's attitudes toward animals that has similar implications. Kellert found that

> *The period from second to fifth grade was most significantly characterized by a major increase in emotional concern and affection for animals. The years between fifth and eighth grades witnessed a dramatic improvement in factual knowledge and cognitive understanding of animals. Finally, the change from eighth to eleventh grade was marked most of all by a major expansion in ethical and ecological concern for animals and the natural environment... These results suggest educational efforts among children six to ten years of age might best focus on the affective realm, mainly emphasizing emotional concern and sympathy for animals.* (Kellert, quoted in Chawla 1988)

Look at the biographies of prominent naturalists and you'll find more support for this emphasis on affective relationships rather than facts during the first half of the elementary school years. In his memoir, *The Naturalist*, Harvard entomologist E. O. Wilson describes his fascination with capturing animals in childhood. He kept a jar of harvester ants under his bed, caught butterflies in homemade cheesecloth nets, made a secret shelter out of poison oak stems that caused a fearful rash, and walked into the house one day with a coachwhip snake wrapped around his neck. Commenting on these early days, he claims,

> *Hands-on experience at the critical time, not systematic knowledge, is what counts in the making of a naturalist. Better to be an untutored savage for a while, not to know the names or anatomical detail. Better to spend long stretches of time just searching and dreaming.* (Wilson 1994)

Instead, in schools and at nature centers, we see just the opposite: science units on animal taxonomy in the third grade where students never go outside; young students being charged with the responsibility of saving endangered species; and a prevailing, Don't touch! attitude when children actually get outside. "Nature is fragile and we have to make sure not to harm her," you'll hear the naturalist caution, advocating for a kind of environmental puritanicalism. We wind up discouraging exactly the behavior that Wilson

says was crucial to his becoming a natural scientist. Our goal, especially through ages nine and ten, should be to foster close allegiances between children and animals. This means playing at being animals, interacting with animals, and taking care of animals. As Brenda Petersen implies, we have to become animals before we can save them.

This is exactly what the Brookfield Zoo near Chicago is trying to do. Brookfield is known as an innovator in the zoo community. Zoo managers have led the way in endangered species protection, in replacing cages with simulated natural habitats for animals, and in thinking seriously about developmental psychology in their exhibit design and education for children. When beginning the process of creating a new children's zoo, administrators agreed that their primary goal was to foster an ethic of care about the natural world in children. Note that this is quite different from educating children about animals. Their literature about the new Hamill Family Play Zoo, aimed at families with children up to ten years old, is clear about their new approach.

> *Wanna come play in the dirt? Pet a boa? Find some worms? Be a veterinarian? Build a nest? Play with bunnies? Groom a dog? Be a monkey?*
>
> *On June 14, 2001, Brookfield Zoo opened the Hamill Family Play Zoo, a revolutionary new concept in zoo experiences for families. The Play Zoo is a unique adventure where children and their families can play and interact with animals, plants, and people to help develop caring attitudes toward the natural world. In this technological age, where children have frequent exposure to computers and television, the Play Zoo is an effort to bring them back to a simpler world and help parents and other caregivers rediscover the magic and importance of playing in nature.*
>
> *This is not your father's Children's Zoo. This is an entirely new concept in zoo experiences for children. Children need to touch, explore, build, do...***The idea is not primarily to educate or inform, but to foster love and caring.*** *Brookfield Zoo wants kids to feel connected with nature. Letting them be in it and care for animals and nature is the best way to do that.* (Brookfield Zoo 2001)

Walking into the Play Zoo is like taking a deep breath of sweet mountain air. It's like slipping on a shoe and having it fit perfectly and comfortably. With deep consciousness and conviction, the zoo staff has integrated a developmental understanding of early childhood with their concerns for animal protection. The result is a unique haven for children and animals. A poster in the bathroom informs parents that "You won't find information about endangered animals in the Family Play Zoo."

In ZooScape Mountain, children explore nooks and crannies that bring them face to face with a variety of animals or lead to places where they can put on animal costumes and become a woodpecker or a lemur. The Animal Hospital is a child-scaled veterinarian's office where children can listen to the pulse of animal puppets, pretend to take X-rays, bandage up injured teddy bears. Sometimes they get to observe real veterinary checkups.

At the Keeper Kitchen, children follow along as the keeper prepares meals for Play Zoo animals. As the Keeper cuts real carrots and bananas, children slice simulated salt dough fruits and vegetables, listening to the Keeper's explanation of what makes good diets for bunnies and monkeys. Then the children accompany the Keeper as she delivers meals. The Play Zoo brochure states, "Dramatic play is not only one of the great joys of childhood, it's also how kids learn to make sense of the world around them. They observe, imitate, and use their imagination to express how animals move, eat, sleep and interact."

As I was strolling through the Workshop where children help to build exhibit trees and boulders and paint signs to be posted throughout the exhibits, one mother commented, "I can't tell you how happy this place makes me. It works for my three-year-old and my ten-year-old. It's just exactly right."

Outside are all the play environments that have disappeared from too many children's lives. There's a playable stream that feels like the Garden of Eden where children can wade, rock-hop, play Pooh sticks, and catch bugs and frogs. In copses of trees you can get up and away into tree forts where you can secretly peer out at birds in the branches around you. My favorite spot is the Animal Homes Adventure Play area, which is the closest thing to European adventure playgrounds that I have seen in this country. With a variety of tools and natural materials (loose parts, in landscape architecture terms) such as branches, leaves, mud, bamboo, straw, and animal hides, children can build their own versions of animal homes. Play Partners, zoo staff committed to playing with children and getting parents to play with their kids, are there with animal puppets to explore the spaces that children create.

Katie Slivovsky, a past senior educator at the zoo, clarifies that the Play Zoo represents a distinct change in approach for the zoo. She recalls a scene from the Elephant House a few years earlier:

> *A female interpreter was in the Elephant House at the zoo talking with a man and his five-year-old son. The boy remarked that the elephants sure have big tusks. The interpreter replied, "Yes, and did you know that elephants are being killed for*

their tusks? The males have the biggest tusks so they're targeted first, then the oldest females are shot, which can really mess things up because the females are in charge and without them, the herds don't know what to do. Killing elephants for their tusks is a huge problem for elephant families."

I wonder what the interpreter really accomplished by talking about elephant poaching with a five-year-old. Though her language was developmentally appropriate, her message was not. How does a child reconcile their feelings of awe and wonder about an animal they're looking at while hearing how its relatives are being shot right and left?

It's not a cop-out to save big, complex issues like poaching, mass habitat destruction and cultural genocide for middle schoolers who are better equipped to handle them. Early and middle childhood is the time to lay the foundation for future caring by providing lots of positive, meaningful, joyful experiences. (2001)

The Brookfield Zoo is successfully loading the ark of the child's mind. By becoming a lemur, a fawn, or a prairie dog, the child internalizes the spirit of each creature. By becoming an animal doctor, a zookeeper, a gardener, the child roughs in an ethic of caring for our animal and plant compatriots. Knowledge is sure to follow.

MAPS &
PATHS
◆

PRINCIPLE 4: MAPS AND PATHS

Finding shortcuts, figuring out what's around the next bend, following a map to a secret event. Children have an inborn desire to explore local geographies. Developing a local sense of place leads organically to a bioregional sense of place and hopefully to biospheric consciousness.

Local and state geography is one of the themes for the fourth-grade curriculum in Waldorf schools. The students go on long walks exploring the neighborhoods around the school and they draw pictorial and panoramic-view maps of this area. At the Monadnock Waldorf School in Keene, New Hampshire, students study the plants and animals of New Hampshire, and each child makes their own raised relief map of the state in preparation for a three-day hiking trip in the White Mountains.

As a parent chaperone for the outing, I drove three of the children up to the mountains. The valley of the Pemigewasset River narrowed as we approached Franconia Notch, and I started to point out some of the mountains they had learned about when they made their maps. Melinda gazed at the sinuous green peaks, got a faraway look in her eyes, and exclaimed, "I know where we are! Remember where the mountains smush in close to the river between two long, low mountains and then the big mountains are just beyond. We're between those low mountains and there's Cannon Mountain and the Franconia Range up there." As she spoke she gestured to show the river valley and ridge forms that she had meticulously shaped with her hands while making her raised relief map. It was fascinating to watch the mapmaking images stored in her hands and mind snap into resolution with the mountain landscape spread out before us. Inner world met outer world in this aha moment of well-crafted curricular experience.

The arduous backpacking, group food preparation, inky night walks, autumnal swims, and wind-whipped view from the top of Cannon Mountain bound everyone together in a spirit of hard-won collaboration. The most awesome experience, however, came in our exploration of a network of boulder caves at the base of the cliffs on the west side of the mountain. For almost an hour the children were like moles on a reconnaissance mission, ferreting out tunnel after tunnel, finding shortcuts from one chamber to another. I encouraged this slightly risky activity because of my conviction that it's this literal immersion and submersion in the rocks, soil, moss, and spruce of the real world that helps root children in their native landscapes. On the other side of the mountain, the stone face of the Old Man of the Mountain used to gaze over the jumbly peaks and valleys of northern New Hampshire. In this rock labyrinth, these students were becoming Children of the Mountains. Getting ready to move on, I gathered everyone beneath one massive boulder and had the children describe their mental maps of this three-dimensional terrain. Again, combining sketches in the soil and convoluted hand and arm gesticulations, they portrayed the multilayered web of passageways.

Although these two examples of mapping are developmentally reversed, they represent just the right scale of pathfinding and mapmaking experiences for upper-elementary-age children. The boulder cave explorations symbolize the "getting to know the neighborhood" phase that should unfold around age nine. This is the beginning of the prime age for path making, and it corresponds with the kinds of challenges experienced by children at this age in hunting and gathering cultures. As young hunters and gatherers moved behind the confines of the camp or village into the bush, their mastery of geographic knowledge was crucial to their survival. Thus, a biologically programmed

fascination with identifying animal signs, tracking animals, understanding trail and drainage networks, and calculating shortcuts comes down to even modern-day children. Our fascination with treasure maps is, I suspect, rooted in the internal maps we developed as hunters and gatherers that led to the true treasure—sustenance.

Beyond the neighborhood, making maps of the community and the wider region happens in incremental steps. The salt-dough maps of New Hampshire prepared the children with anticipatory images of the backpacking trip they were about to go on. And the view from the top of the mountain looked not unlike the crenulated landscapes they'd created with their own hands. By honoring the developmental unfolding of geographic understanding, this teacher rooted the children's learning in the local landscape.

One of my favorite examples of developing a sense of place through mapmaking was a yearlong project in Steve Moore's fourth-grade classroom in Springfield, Vermont. Realizing that the study of "Vermont history and geography" as required in the curriculum frameworks was too tall an order for his fourth graders, Steve instead decided to focus on the Black River watershed. The river runs through the center of Springfield on its way from the Green Mountains to the Connecticut River. Springfield was home to a machine-tools industry, and the river was dammed and harnessed for hydropower, making for lots of industrial buildings, alleyways, raging torrents, and other explorable nooks and crannies just a couple of minutes from Steve's classroom.

Over the course of the year, he took the students on numerous walking field trips to explore the banks of the river, the architecture, and the industrial heritage of the city. They mapped their playgrounds and made sketch maps of walks from their school to the river. One field trip took them to the beginnings of the river, where the students could hop across the headwaters in a single bound. Another trip worked students down to the mouth of the river. Here, the students could toss a stone only a tiny fraction of the way across the river. These mapmaking and kinesthetic experiences ingrained the concept of watershed structure in their muscles as well as their minds.

Steve discovered a book containing the journal of a ten-year-old boy growing up in Springfield in the 1920s. Excerpts from this journal became part of the literature base of the project. During this long-ago fourth-grade experience, one of the major bridges across the river was under construction so children had to turn off Main Street down a narrow dark alley and pass over the spring-flood waterfall turbulence of the river on a rickety pedestrian footbridge. What fun it was for these fourth-graders to slink down the same alleyway and imagine this harrowing crossing.

In the spring, after getting to know the river and city on foot, the students came back to class one day to find two doors lined up horizontally on a frame in the center of the classroom. Each child received an eleven-by-seven-inch black and white photo enlargement of the buildings along the river. "Imagine these doors are the river flowing through the city," Steve explained. "Where there's a gap between the doors is the water-fall in the center of the city. Line yourselves up along the banks of the river according to where the building you have in your hands should be."

The students had explored this area enough so they could re-create the structures along both banks of the river. Two girls commented, "You forgot the bridge!" so they held hands across the waterfall where the bridge was located. Steve then gave them their task. "Our job is to make a model of the river and the center of Springfield, from the upper dam, past the waterfall to the lower dam. Each of you will be responsible for re-creating your own building and then we'll all have jobs helping to create the river and its banks."

Over the next three weeks, the classroom was an active construction site. To build the bridge, Steve helped the two girls build a form, laying wire to simulate reinforcing bar, and then mixed up a batch of cement to pour into the form. It was the ultimate manifestation of the progressive education dictum to make the curriculum concrete. Each child researched and built her own industrial building out of cardboard and other suitable materials. These were constructed along the edges of the doors, which became the banks of the river. Steve took the students on a field trip to a tiny stream where he had built a little dam to power a miniature water turbine. Here he could simulate the hydropower facilities inside many of the buildings being reconstructed by the students. On the way back, students collected slate from the edge of the river, which they split once back in the classroom to line the banks of the model. Whenever there was a question about the number of windows, or the location of a trail, it went onto a list, to be answered during the next walking field trip.

When they were done, the students had created a fifteen-foot-long, attractively painted miniature world in their classroom. (Think back to Cobb's notion that what children want most is to make a world in which to find a place to discover a self.) The creation of the model was the culminating project for the yearlong study of the water-shed. Through reading local literature, making scale models, understanding why the mills closed down, and studying the physics of waterpower, the project integrated read-ing, math, social studies, and science, and could be seen as a metaphor for their learn-ing: All that developmentally appropriate activity—path following, stream jumping, and poking around in industrial basements—was the waterpower. The model making

(essentially, a three-dimensional map) was a turbine that transformed the waterpower into usable energy—learning about Vermont history and geography.

In Colorado, high school students have mapped car accident sites for use by emergency rescue teams. In Vermont, Rivendell High School students are mapping and building a hiking trail to connect four towns in a newly created interstate school district. In Brooklyn, New York, students produced a map of local toxic waste sites as part of a community initiative to reduce asthma in children. When harnessed appropriately, children's fascination with mapmaking can be a powerful learning tool.

SPECIAL
PLACES

PRINCIPLE 5: SPECIAL PLACES

Almost everyone remembers a fort, den, tree house, or hidden corner in the back of a closet. Especially between ages eight and eleven, children like to find and create places where they can hide away and retreat into their own found or constructed spaces.

My family and friends all know that I'm always looking for the perfect place. The best picnic spot with a mondo view of the mountain in the shade of a big white pine with easily pickable blueberries and no bugs. The swimming hole that not many people know about with a gravelly beach and a fifteen-foot ledge jump into deep, green water. The little Italian place in the North End of Boston that seats only thirty people and serves the best parmigiana. The restored saltwater farm all alone at the end of a dirt road on an island off the coast of Maine that puts the glisten on summer family vacations. Each place sits at the optimal intersection of a set of variables.

My favorite fort-building place is a wild coastline with big piles of storm-driven driftwood and nobody in sight for miles. A true Robinson Crusoe setting. My children and their friends and I have found these places on Drakes Beach on Pt. Reyes National Seashore north of San Francisco, in Tamarindo on the Pacific Coast of Costa Rica, on Frenchboro on the outer reaches of Penobscot Bay in Maine. The jumbo piles of broken lobster traps, weathered boat siding, dock pilings, shed roofs, plastic buoy line, and dismembered beach stairs provide just the right raw materials for crafting driftwood cottages. In describing optimal play spaces for children, landscape architect Samuel Nicholson articulated the theory of "loose parts" indicating that, "In any environment, both the degree of inventiveness and creativity, and the possibility of discovery, are directly proportional to the number and kind of variables in it" (1971). In other words, children like play settings where there are lots of things to do and lots of "loose parts" to use to create new structures or be transformed into horses, swords, kitchenware, or furniture. The flotsam and jetsam of driftwood piles are to fort building as Legos are to futuristic space jets.

On the outer beach at Cape Cod we crafted the perfect shelter with driftwood boards to protect us from the wind-driven sand one breezy May day. On Frenchboro, my son and I remodeled a cottage with a great picture window and a crow's nest roof perch. He worked on the walkway while I rebuilt the front wall with thick, flat slabs of granite. A friend of mine, knowing my appreciation of children's special places, sent me an article about the beach forts of Cuttyhunk, off the coast of Massachusetts. This colony of forts had become a permanent fixture of the island's summer population. They were multiroomed shelters with porches, dining rooms, and bedrooms, where legions of eight- to thirteen-year-old boys spent the night playing cards and giggling. Their ownership passed from older to younger boys as social interests emerged in adolescence. They were a testimony to the creative place-making spirit of indigenous young architects making do with the *loose parts* provided by the sea.

In *Children's Special Places*, published in 1992, I described what appears to be a universal tendency for children to create or find their own private places, especially between the ages of approximately seven and twelve. I believe the creation of these places serves many developmental purposes for children. The fort is a home away from home in nature; it provides a bridge between the safe, protected world of the family and the independent self in the wider world of adolescence. These places also serve as vehicles of bonding with the natural world, allowing children to feel comfortable in the landscape, connected to it, and eventually committed to acting as stewards of it. At that time, I focused mostly on individually and group-created places in children's neighborhoods, and somewhat less on schoolground forts. (See *Children's Special Places* [1992] and *Mapmaking with Children* [1998] for numerous examples of special-place-inspired curriculum ideas.) Since then, many child-savvy teachers and psychologists have provided opportunities for children to construct and maintain villages of schoolground forts. Their experiences point the way to understanding the learning potential of allowing children to act out their innermost desires.

SCHOOLYARD FORTS

Over the past decade, outdoor play has continued to disappear from the landscape of childhood. Increased emphasis on youth sports means there's little unstructured time

after school for backyard play. The increased frequency of two working parents also means that when there is unstructured time, children are required to stay inside or in a supervised child-care situation. In urban areas, pollution, inadequate waste management, drug trafficking, and street violence make parents hesitant to let children engage in neighborhood play. Highly publicized abductions of children also make parents fearful. "I don't dare let them out of my sight," many parents confess.

Thus, schoolyards, where there's adequate supervision and sometimes the right resources, provide one of the few opportunities for children to make special places and build forts. I've been fascinated to observe that when the right ingredients exist, schoolyard villages will spontaneously pop into existence. It's like making fire: when you've got some nice dry leaves, the sun is high in the sky, and you hold the magnifying glass at just the right angle, just the right distance from the leaf surface, poof—a little flame appears.

What are the just-right elements for schoolyard forts?

- twenty or more children aged seven to twelve

- a wooded area adjacent to the school building or playground that is accessible to the children (if the woods are off limits, nothing happens)

- enough "loose parts" to be used in construction (this is usually branches, fallen trees, or old brush piles, but can also be scrap wood from a construction project)

- an open-minded faculty and administration who understand the value of children's exploratory play in the woods

All these ingredients have to be present for schoolyard forts to materialize. More often, these conditions occur at independent elementary schools, but I have seen forts arise on the grounds of public schools where there's a deep appreciation of outdoor play.

In the past ten years in the Monadnock region of southwestern New Hampshire, a number of public school teachers have used the special places impulse to structure curriculum. When she taught at the Temple Elementary School, Mickey Johnson had her third graders create a class-sized special place out in the woods behind the school. This became a gathering spot for special class meetings, storytelling, and some science classes. From here, the children were encouraged to make their own individual special places, not far from the class place, where they would go for journal-writing assignments. Other teachers have followed this model, having their children create special places that they visit recurrently for quiet work. I can't tell you how many teachers have said, "At the end of the year, when I ask the children what they liked best in the curriculum, many of them commented that they loved reading, writing, or being alone in their special place." Through recognizing children's deep impulses and building on them, the curriculum can be enhanced.

Schoolyard villages, however, come completely from the children. If they are allowed to flourish, they can become a major component in the life of the school. Mark Powell (2001), an elementary teacher at the Lexington Montessori School in Lexington, Massachusetts, conducted one of the most comprehensive studies of this phenomenon. His findings suggest some of the potential values and pitfalls of schoolyard villages.

> *Fort play at Lexington Montessori School (LMS) is a primarily social activity that is collectively constructed, owned and negotiated at recess and beyond through a culture generated entirely from the spontaneous interests of children. This peer culture of fort play, with its rules and roles, has been passed down to succeeding generations of students as they enter the elementary program since it began at its present site in 1990. From interviews with and surveys of both alumni and current students, it is clear that for the majority of children at LMS, the culture of fort play available at recess has been a significant part of their overall learning experience at the school. For these children, recess was not simply a break from the "real" learning that took place in the classroom. For many former students, fort play was one of the most prominent and positive memories of all their years at the school. The appeal of this activity for children derives in general from its free-ranging nature, from the control it gives them over their interactions with each other and with the natural environment.*

The fort area at LMS is adjacent to the soccer field and the large-play and climbing structure. As many as a dozen stick forts exist at any one time. They are either built or maintained by members of the fort, generally ranging from two to five children. Ownership of the fort, the materials it is made of, and the territory surrounding the fort are crucial elements of fort culture. The difference between individual backyard forts and schoolyard forts is the complex social dynamic that emerges around social hierarchy, in-group differentiation, and shared resources. It's like the difference between living in an isolated summer place on the lake and living in an apartment building. At the forts at LMS, life was not always a bowl of cherries. "Arguments between and within fort groups over rules, roles, resources such as sticks, and the right to exclude 'non-members'

were for many years the major source of conflict between children at the school" (Powell 2001). As a limited resource, sticks were often stolen by members of one fort to be used on other forts. Bickering would often emerge over who could be a member of the fort, what the responsibilities of membership were, and under what conditions someone could be kicked out of the fort.

In order to deal with the ongoing petty conflicts regarding the forts, the faculty stepped in and helped the children create a set of rules to govern fort behavior in 1995. I have seen this happen in a variety of settings: it parallels the history of civilization. Like the emergence of the Magna Carta in England, or the framing of the Constitution, cultures, as they evolve, recognize the need to codify behavior and create a legal system. In the evolution of schoolyard villages, if children can't do this on their own, it's contingent upon the faculty to step in and use this as a learning opportunity. (In many schoolyard villages, a currency spontaneously arises as well and is used for transactions that were previously conducted through a barter system. What a great opportunity for economics education!) Out of this faculty-student convocation came The Ultimate, Absolute Fort Rules (Powell 2001). Excerpts from some of the rules follow:

- It is okay to keep a fort, materials, or a location from year to year, but you must identify the fort, materials, or location (by initials, neat piles of materials, a flag or another symbol).

- If materials are traded, both forts must be involved and at the trading session. If a fort wants to use another fort's sticks, they must ask and be friendly.

- Forts need to tell kids what the rules are before they join. They should also find out what fort a person wanting to join was in before in case s/he is a spy.

- A person can be fired from a fort after a day if s/he has not obeyed the rules of the fort, if s/he understands why s/he is being asked to leave and if all members of the fort agree. Fort wreckers can be fired right away under the same conditions.

- Fort land must be limited to up to twenty feet all around the fort when there is that much space available. This limit should be from the main part of the fort rather than from individual sticks which are placed outside of the main walls. Treaties can be made between forts for more land.

I have quoted extensively from The Ultimate, Absolute Fort Rules to indicate the richness of the potential social learning inherent in the fort culture. Piaget considers cognitive disequilibrium as a precondition for learning. The tensions inherent in competition for resources, and questions regarding inclusion and exclusion are rife with cognitive disequilibrium and offer rich learning opportunities. Clearly, the creation of the rules modeled the process of policy development or of writing legislation. Is there any better way for children to learn about state government (often part of mandated fourth-grade curriculum) than to deal with a comparable challenge of developing rules that will shape how citizens of the community will behave?

Similarly, the study of United States and European history would be enriched with these issues used as prototypes. The rule regarding land owned around the fort can be used as an analogy for understanding the territorial claims of countries regarding fishing rights within specified distances from the shore of that country. Guidelines for trading of sticks can be used to illustrate the problems of European imperialism and the practice of claiming "unclaimed" land from indigenous cultures in the Americas and Africa. And the spontaneous evolution of currencies provides the opportunity to discuss why cultures evolved from barter to hard currency systems and to get at that enduring puzzle of What is money, anyway? Why does money have value?

In his study at LMS, Mark Powell (2001) also recommends that the school "Implement conflict resolution instruction and peer mediation." He explains,

> *Open hostility between fort groups at LMS has probably declined since its height in the mid-1990s. Over the last few years there appears to have been a cultural shift in fort play away from its previous focus on interfort "war" and the accumulation of sticks at the expense of other groups toward more peaceful and social activities. However, there remains considerable frustration among fort players over how to negotiate the rules and roles of fort play both between and within forts.*

Here's a ready-made opportunity for peer mediation training in schools. I have often been skeptical about the peer-mediation craze and the training of fifth- and sixth-grade mediators in schools. Sometimes, it feels like teachers are abnegating their responsibilities and dumping an adult burden on children's shoulders. And the problems that children are expected to mediate often emerge out of abusive family interactions, socioeconomic and cultural differences, and emotional problems that are far beyond the student mediator's understanding. In this case, however, the resource and territory problems are concrete and tangible, and the social dynamics tend to be more limited in scope, so it's an appropriate scale and context for student mediation. This would also be a great way to understand the whole idea behind a U.N. Peacekeeping Force.

SPECIAL PLACES AND SUSTAINABILITY

An innovative school in Costa Rica has pioneered a way to connect the special places impulse with ecological stewardship behavior. The Cloud Forest School is a K through 12 bilingual school mostly serving the native Costa Rican families in Santa Elena and Monteverde, high montane agricultural communities bordering a large tropical forest reserve. In the last fifty years, Monteverde has developed a substantial ecotourism economy based on scientific research, ornithology, and natural history recreation. One of the core goals of the school is to develop students who are committed to sustainably preserving the cultural and ecological integrity of their communities. Through a relationship with the Nature Conservancy, the school acquired more than one hundred acres of agricultural land bordering the forest reserve, with the understanding that the land would be restored with ecological integrity.

In 2004, the school's land manager, Milton Brenes, and environmental education co-coordinator Karen Gordon established a Special Places project on a section of the school property designated for reforestation. The idea was to reforest the pastureland to create corridors of forest, thereby expanding wildlife habitat and converting the land back to its native ecology.

To get the project rolling, each third- and fourth-grade student was gifted a five-by-ten-meter plot of pastureland. In August, students spent an hour a week getting to know the unique features of their Special Place through mapping and creative writing exercises. The school newsletter describes:

> *Niko Walker, a 3rd grader, had an exciting moment when he came upon an emerald toucanet bill in his plot. As he shared his discovery with his classmates, questions arose such as, "Why do you think it was found in this area and not in another? What do you think happened to the toucanet?" Using this teachable moment in Niko's special place, the students entered into a truly engaged conversation with one another, sharing their hypotheses, knowledge, and appreciation for the emerald toucanet.* (Gordon and Brenes 2005)

Next, the children prepared their plots for tree planting by removing African stargrass and other invasive plants—lots of sweaty spadework in rootbound soil with shovels that were as tall as the students. Once the ground was cleared and cultivated, the plots were planted with fourteen species of native trees. The students had learned the distinctive natural history of each of the species. By November, over 300 trees had been planted.

From January through March the curriculum focused on studying the cloud-forest ecosystem, with academic subjects concretized through observations and activities in the special places. Teachers led math lessons that required students to monitor the growth of their trees. Science and language arts journaling activities in adjacent forested land provided images of the habitat they were trying to create. The teachers claim, "Perhaps the most valuable lesson being ingrained is that the forest can come back—in this case because the students have been there and have done the work" (Gordon and Brenes 2005).

In a world where tropical rain forest is being cut down at the rate of an acre a minute, it's heartening to see students involved in reforestation in their backyards. And the intriguing aspect here is the special places starting point. Through using children's native tendency to bond with a small piece of land, the teachers build a sense of connectedness that starts small and gradually, hopefully, expands to the whole of the montane cloud forest and eventually to all of Costa Rica. Just think what could happen if this was an integral aspect of all schooling.

The special places impulse in a school setting invites children to relive the history of the species. They create primitive shelters, form tribes, battle over resources, learn to barter, create legal systems, invent currency, learn to monitor their own behavior, recognize the impact of the built environment on the natural environment, learn to restore changed ecosystems. This could be the basis of the whole social studies curriculum for the upper elementary school. If your students start to build stick forts on the edge of the playground, don't discourage them.

SMALL
WORLDS
◆

PRINCIPLE 6: SMALL WORLDS

From sand boxes to doll houses to model train sets, children love to create miniature worlds that they can play inside of. Through creating miniature representations of ecosystems, or neighborhoods, we help children conceptually grasp the big picture. The creation of small worlds provides a concrete vehicle for understanding abstract ideas.

Drive up Route 1, heading Down East, and then turn south down one of those long fingers of rock that stick out into the drowned coastline of the Gulf of Maine. In Port Clyde, catch the mailboat for the hour-and-a-half ride out to Monhegan Island. Take Dramamine an hour before departure if you have any tendency toward seasickness. It's often rough. Once you're off the boat, ask anyone, really anyone, how to get to Fairyland in the Cathedral Woods. Then keep your eyes open. Fairies are good at integrated architecture, making sure their structures blend effortlessly into the hummocky spruce and fir forest floor. The cottages, cabins, gardens, walkways, tree lookouts, and elevated walkways are always there and always changing. Fairyland has become such an accepted part of the island culture that someone is always creating a new hideout, or repairing storm damage to existing castles.

Fairyland is a testimony to the widespread appeal of miniature worlds. Think of the lavish train layout at the Germany exhibit in Epcot at Disney World, or the fastidiously to-scale version of the Netherlands at Madurodam, or Bradford Washburn's elegant model of Mt. Everest at the Boston Museum of Science. On vacation on a historically intact island off the coast of New England one summer, my daughter commented that it felt like living inside one of those museum dioramas of what the village looked like in the nineteenth century. Which is, of course, exactly what we would all like to do—take the Eat Me cookie from *Alice in Wonderland* and shrink ourselves down so we can go inside the model.

Small worlds work wonders for children. They provide the same kind of emotional security that islands provide for vacationers. The world is simplified and knowable. They provide cognitive accessibility because all the disparate elements of a place are brought into one view. It's like the one-page organizational chart for the organization, the site map for the website, the logic model that describes the underlying assumptions for a project. You look at the chart and think, "Oh, now I see how it all fits together."

The problem with lots of nature education, or really with lots of any kind of education, is that it gets too big, or too abstract, too fast. If we could just abide by the turtle's guiding wisdom that slow and steady wins the race, we'd be doing much better on those international tests of science and math aptitude. Steve Moore's model of the center of Springfield was both a mapping project and a small-world project, allowing the students to see the structure of the city all at a glance. This all-at-a-glance principle works at each developmental level. Therefore, let me share examples of using small worlds to teach plant communities with fifth graders and to teach sustainable design with teachers.

ON THE BEACH

The year after my daughter's class went to the White Mountains, they headed to the Rhode Island coast for a week. One of the topics in the fifth-grade curriculum is botany and plant communities, so as a contributing parent I took on the challenge of teaching the children seaside botany and barrier-beach plant communities. My goal was to get children to be able to see that as you move from the beach to the foredune to the back dune to the swale to the salt marsh edge, there are different constellations of plants adapted to different amounts of wind, salt exposure, sunlight, and fresh water availability.

First, we learned about poison ivy. It grows rampantly and prolifically in sandy soil on the southern New England coast, and since we were going to do lots of poking around in the dunes collecting plants, it was important for them to recognize poison ivy in all its guises. That done, everyone went out and collected six sprigs of the most common plants they could find in different areas. We gathered back together, sorted them into groups of things that were alike, and then I identified what we had and the unique character of each plant. Pioneering beach grass grows on the foredune, its long rhizome roots stabilizing the dunes. Seaside rose, with those gigantic sweet rose hips, is a bit less adventurous, growing in the back dune where there's a bit of protection from the wind. In the swale, where there's even more protection and fresh water, there's bayberry, an early source of candle wax for salt marsh farmers. To create a limited universe, I decided that we would focus on the fifteen most prominent plants, one plant for each child in the class. Each child had to do a detailed botanical drawing of their plant, and everyone was responsible for being able to identify and learn the names of all fifteen plants. It took us a couple of days of botanizing, drawing, and diverse name games to get them all straight.

The next morning, we found a copse of pitch pines and I portrayed the challenge. We had been botanizing a section of dunes and salt marsh that stretched about two hundred meters from ocean beach to salt marsh edge. From any one place, it was hard to see the whole stretch, but we had rambled through all the plant communities.

Your mission, should you choose to accept it, is to create a small world showing the different plants that grow in different places from beach to salt marsh edge. The idea is to show the handful of plants that are most particular to the different places we've been exploring. Your little world or model should be no more than six feet from one

end to the other and you should represent the plants so that they are approximately in scale with your landscape. In other words, the beach grass shouldn't tower over the dunes, and since beach grass is about three feet tall and pine trees are about fifteen feet tall, the pine trees should be about five times bigger than the beach grass.

With little hesitation, they set to work creating miniature dunes, wooden walkways, copses of trees that the fairies on Monhegan would die for. I loved watching them look down on their models, then look out to survey the back dune or the swale, and then reach down to adjust the shape of the dune or move some plants. With little prior conversation about which plants belonged where, they all re-created fairly accurate groupings of representative plants. They were the kinds of dioramas you wanted to shrink into and explore. Presenting their models, they could all articulate why they located different constellations of plants in different locations. To assess their understanding of the character of different plants, I asked them each to choose the plant they would want to be and explain how the personality of the plant is similar to some aspect of their personality. "I'd be a cranberry because I like to stay a little hidden and I can be kind of sour." "I'd be Pearly Everlasting because I like to bake in the sun and get lots of fresh air." I was amazed at both their plant knowledge and their ability to project themselves into this habitat. That evening, I drew a very sketchy diagram on the board and assigned them to do colorful diagrams of the plants in each of the four major zones. Their elegant illustrations demonstrated the depth of their learning.

I attribute the success of this learning sequence to the sequence of the activities and the cognitive appropriateness of the final small-world construction challenge. The challenge of miniaturizing a two-hundred-meter chunk of landscape down to two meters was just right. The two hundred meters had just enough diversity, and the two meters was big enough to give them space to be creative. Then, with the small-world models as a transitional metaphor, it worked to go the next step onto paper. We translated a large three-dimensional space into a small three-dimensional model and then into a two-dimensional abstracted form. Later in the year, the teacher could use this concept of plant zonation to talk about changing plant communities as you climb up a mountain or as you travel from New England to the North Pole.

SMALL WORLDS AND SUSTAINABILITY

I used the same principle for a teacher workshop at the Islandwood Environmental Learning Center on Bainbridge Island, near Seattle, Washington. Islandwood is one of the most sensitively designed residential environmental education facilities in the country. The siting of the residential buildings, dormitories, trails, study areas, and stream restoration projects was the result of a very sophisticated land-use planning process. Using a system pioneered by Ian McHarg, planners created separate overlay transparency maps that identified wildlife distributions, slope, soil permeability, floristic communities, forest health and age, and other parameters. By laying the transparencies on top of each other it became clear where the buildings should be located (mild slopes, good soil permeability, recently logged sections) and which areas should be preserved in their current state (intact ecological communities, resident wildlife). This process gives the land a voice so it can tell us how best to work with it.

This process is emblematic of Islandwood's goal to model sustainable development, systems thinking, and the development of ecological literacy in students and teachers. I was asked to do a teacher workshop before any facilities were developed, just as the initial land clearing and road construction were going on. Since designing with nature was such an integral part of the center's ethic, I decided to translate this process into a teacher-workshop activity using the small-worlds design principle.

Prior to the teachers' arrival, I chose an area of forest with interesting microtopography and only small amounts of herbs and shrubs. I laid out study plots that measured four feet by six feet. Each plot had some flat spots and some steep slopes, vegetated areas, and open areas. I provided a base map with the boundaries of their plots identified and asked them to create overlay maps that identified soil permeability, slope, and vegetation. I provided spoons and stop watches to dig test pits and measure water percolation rates, meter sticks and levels to measure slopes, and identification guides of local flora. Once the three transparencies were complete, the maps were overlaid and then the teachers had to decide where to site the educational facilities, where to install a septic system, and where to locate an interpretive trail. Wooden blocks to represent buildings and signage materials amplified the small-worlds opportunities.

The teachers had a ball and they learned a lot about sustainable design. Many had no idea what a percolation test was, nor what the issues were regarding siting septic systems. Our discussions about not siting structures on steep slopes led to conversations about land-use planning-code restrictions in erosion-prone areas. Everyone had a deepened appreciation of the ecological thoughtfulness that went into the center's decision-making. Through using a small-worlds approach, we took the abstract ideas of sustainability and ecological design and made them accessible to classroom teachers. Whereas the Rhode Island example focused on geographic and botanical learning, here I was aspiring to make visible a much more conceptually abstract way

of thinking. The same children and nature design principle can be used effectively at different developmental levels.

PRINCIPLE 7:
HUNTING AND GATHERING

From a genetic perspective, we are still hunting and gathering organisms. Gathering and collecting anything compels us; searching for hidden treasure or the Holy Grail is a recurrent mythic form. Look at the success of Where's Waldo. How do we design learning opportunities like treasure hunts?

Try this test. Read the following passage and try to predict the character of this boy as an adult. Would he be someone you would want your child playing with after school?

One of our amusements was hunting cats without seriously hurting them...One time in particular I remember, when we began throwing stones at an experienced old Tom, not wishing to hurt him much, though he was a tempting mark...I happened to strike him pretty hard with a good-sized pebble, but he still blinked and sat still as if without feeling. "He must be mortally wounded," I said, "and now we must kill him to put him out of his pain," the savage in us rapidly growing with indulgence. All took heartily to this sort of cat mercy and began throwing the heaviest stones we could manage, but that old fellow knew what characters we were, and suddenly with a wild whirr and gurr of energy, he launched himself over our heads... and over the garden wall.

Our most exciting sport, however, was playing with gunpowder. We made guns out of gas-pipe, mounted them on sticks of any shape, clubbed our pennies together for powder, gleaned pieces of lead here and there and cut them into slugs, and, while one aimed, another applied a match to the touch-hole. With these awful weapons, we wandered along the beach and fired at the gulls and solan-geese as they passed us. Fortunately we never hurt any of them that we knew of. We also dug holes in the ground, put in a handful or two of powder, tamped it well around a fuse made of a wheat-stalk, and, reaching cautiously forward, touched a match to the straw. This we called making earthquakes. Oftentimes we went home with singed hair and faces well peppered with powder-grains that could not be washed out.

This boy secretively crept around on steep, slate roofs after being put to bed, regularly got into fights, stole young skylarks from their nests to hand raise them, and got into all kinds of trouble. Sound like just the kind of ruffian you'd rather not have your son associate with? Then he would have missed hunting and adventuring with John Muir, who describes these escapades in *The Story of My Boyhood and Youth* (1913).

Look back at Bob Pyle's and E. O. Wilson's accounts of their boyhoods. Remember that John James Audubon was an avid bird collector, Aldo Leopold a thoughtful hunter. Many great naturalists and environmentalists enjoyed boyhoods that included a substantial amount of hunting. In light of the fact that we still retain the genetic structure of our hunting and gathering ancestors, it's not surprising that young boys and girls intuitively play at games that were an integral part of preagrarian lifestyles for thousands and thousands of years.

On the island of Carriacou, just north of Grenada in the Caribbean, I stumbled into a children's culture that still preserved many of these elements about twenty years ago. I was taking a year's leave of absence from my teaching job to enjoy family time and research children's relationships with their environments. We spent half of the year in Devon, England, and the other half on Carriacou, an undeveloped, untouristed, back-of-beyond kind of place. My research approach was to ask children to make maps of their neighborhoods and then have some of those children take me on field trips to the important places in their nearby geographic territory.

When the field trips started, it was like stepping back in time. The boys took me on hunting expeditions. On the way home from school with the girls, I collected wild cherries or the seedpods of tamarinds. In a mixed group of boys and girls one Saturday morning, we collected sea urchins and ate their roe, tried to spear crayfish and moray eels, shook palm trees to loosen the ripe coconuts so we could drink their milk, and climbed way out on scraggly branches to collect star fruit. Along the way we also sang, played jump rope games, rolled hoops. Their conventional childhood play was interspersed with hunting and gathering activities that were both functional and recreational. Functional because the fish and animals they caught and the fruit they collected served to amplify their meager diets.

Three different hunting expeditions with boys illustrate how hunting was central to their everyday lives. One day after school, two boys decided to take me bird hunting. After dropping off their book bags at home, Matthew grabbed a piece of twine and his pocketknife and led us into the backyard. Here, Josiah and Matthew cut straight branches off an acacia shrub and quickly fabricated bows with the twine. Next, they cut shorter branches, sliced stout thorns from an ocotillo cactus, notched the tips of

the branches and adhered the thorns with a sticky sap, and, voilà! we had arrows. We stalked quietly through the bush, watching the ground for recent bird scratchings, pausing to listen attentively for wing flutter and distant cooing. Within an hour, we had two ground doves. Matthew's mother was happy to add them to their pigeon peas and rice dinner that night.

Two weeks later, I went with a group of boys, age five to twelve, to trap birds. Hollie, the oldest boy, performed like he had his Eagle Scout badge in indigenous hunting techniques. Again, using only twine and a pocketknife and twigs of various shapes and thickness, he and the other boys fabricated delicate snares. When the bird approached the seed left as bait, its pecking dislodged the carefully frictioned trigger, the flying stick snapped skyward, and the bird's leg was snatched up in the loop of twine that encircled its leg. Each boy made his own snare, even five-year-old Boyd. His snare didn't really work, but it was fascinating to watch the older boys patiently help him learn each step of the process. The technique had clearly been passed down from older boys to younger boys over many generations.

One Saturday morning, I climbed Cabesair, an eight-hundred-foot haughty prom-ontory that loomed over the village, like the mountain in *Fantasia*, with another group of boys. From the top, we dropped down a steep cactus and acacia talus slope to a grove of large juniper and mapoo trees. "We find iguana here," Hollie whispered as we got close. Once they sighted one high in the tree, they became a well-organized team with differentiated roles and responsibilities—a scout, a climber, stone throwers stationed on the ground. The climber had to balance his way out a skinny branch, probably thirty feet above the ground, to strike the lizard with a club. Meanwhile the stone throwers distracted it, peppering it from below. It was no match for their organized efficiency.

As it lay dead on the ground, they inspected it with reverence, examining its bleached scales, the ticks attached to its underparts, its fearsome demeanor. Kenroy imitated the imperial glare of the iguana as he stared down from the tree. He rolled his eyes back in his head and you could almost see the row of sawlike prickers rise on his sweaty black back as he arched like the iguana. He pawed the air with his arms to show the way the iguana tried to swim out of the tree before he succumbed. They were proud of their hunting prowess. Their families ate the iguana for dinner that evening.

On a walk up a dry wash in the bush one afternoon with three girls we came upon a massive tamarind tree. Its palm-sized seedpods littered the ground. Placing one on a flat stone and using another round stone as a pounder, Monica cracked one open and the girls hungrily stuffed the yellow-green peanut-buttery pulp into their mouths. Then, as if someone else might show up any minute and steal their discovery, the girls excitedly stuffed their pockets with their prize and made pouches with their dresses to carry home as many as possible. At school they next day they ruled over the playground as they dispensed their riches to the fawning crowds or traded for other valuables.

What's the point of these stories? Am I trying to get published in *Field and Stream*? Am I organizing a Euell Gibbons retrospective? Perhaps both. The impulse to hunt and gather is still very alive in children's psyches. Capture the Flag, Hide-and-Seek, and Kick the Can are all essentially predator/prey games. Sea-glass collections adorn many children's bedrooms. If we recognize that hunting and gathering still exert a strong magnetic pull on children, we can use them to enliven children's learning about the world.

We can do this in both literal and figurative ways. The traditional hunter, prior to the invention of firearms, was an attuned, sophisticated observer of the natural world. Without these skills, he would fail as a hunter. In *Indian Boyhood*, Charles Eastman describes his Sioux childhood in the latter part of the nineteenth century.

> *It was part of our hunting to find new and strange things in the woods. We examined the slightest sign of life; and if a bird had scratched the leaves off the ground, or a bear dragged up a root for his morning meal, we stopped to speculate on the time it was done. If we saw a large old tree with some scratches on its bark, we concluded that a bear or some raccoons must be living there... An old deer-track would at once bring on a warm discussion as to whether it was the track of a buck or a does. Generally, at noon, we met and compared our game, noting at the same time the peculiar characteristics of everything we had killed. It was not merely a hunt, for we combined with it the study of animal life. (1971)*

Designed with recognition that this spirit is alive in children, Keith Badger of the High Mowing School in Wilton, New Hampshire, adapted his year-round field ecology program for high school students into a summer camp experience for nine- to thirteen-year-olds. The Way of the Naturalist teaches children the traditional skills of surviving in the wilderness, including tracking and hunting small game, gathering wild edibles, making fire, and orienteering. Eight summers ago, my son participated in these programs. I was most impressed watching all the children make handmade bows. Using traditional Native American techniques, Keith had cut the six-foot white ash staffs in the winter and then set them to dry for six months. Then each child worked laboriously, first with a drawknife, then with files, to achieve just the right thinness and taper. When

complete, they were strung with sinew, and then each child was trained in the appropriate use of this potentially dangerous weapon. If a child chose to hunt, it was clear that one hunted only if one intended to eat the animal and use its skin appropriately.

To make fires, children were taught two techniques—starting fires with flint and steel or with the use of bow drills. Neither of these came easily, especially because they had to make their own bow drills, but they'd labor for hours to get just the right technique. Figuring out the right angle for striking the flint against the steel, getting just the right kind of flammable material for the spark to land in, learning to blow with the right force once an ember started to glow. What a thrill when the first flame actually appeared!

It was a joy to pick up my son and his best friend each day after their exploits in the woods. They eagerly talked about the day's activities:

> *We were so lost today! Keith took us way far away and dropped us off and we had to find our way back to camp. In the beginning I was really scared and we were all arguing. But eventually, we sat down with the map and compass and remembered what we were supposed to do, and we figured it out. We came out of the woods on the road only about a hundred yards from the camp!*
>
> *Today we ate grasshoppers. We collected them in the field and then brought them back and fried them in some oil over the fire. I was grossed out and swore I wouldn't eat any. But Keith popped a couple in his mouth and Ryan tried one and said they were OK so I tried one, and, you know what? They were good, kind of like popcorn.*

For a period of time when he was around ten years old, my son, Eli, was fascinated with making fires. He had his own little fire kit in a little red plastic toolbox—his flint and steel, some tinder, matches, a lighter, candles. I built a fire pit in the backyard so he had a safe place to ply his craft. He got particularly good at getting fires going in the rain, and I came to depend on him when I needed to get brush fires going. One autumn night he went out to the fire pit after dinner and returned a couple of hours later. "It was so beautiful out there," he said. "Just the darkness, the stars, and the fire. I thought I'd be scared and lonely out there all by myself, but it was really cozy. It was almost as if the fire was my friend."

Isn't this what we want, this sense of friendship between the natural world and our children? It's so easy to take all the risk and solitude out of our children's lives—don't play with matches, don't go out there alone, no you can't use your pocketknife unless you're with an adult. Instead, we need to follow their instinctual hunting and gathering predispositions and use them as the basis for skill development. Tom Brown's Tracker programs, Boy and Girl Scouts, Outward Bound, and National Outdoor Leadership School (NOLS) courses for adolescents are all based on preserving the old ways that live, nascent, inside us.

It's also useful to use the hunting and gathering motif figuratively, to capitalize on the thrill of the quest, the search for the elusive. Unfurl the treasure map slowly. The aged paper threatens to crumble in your hands if you don't exercise the utmost care. Lay it out on the table, rocks placed gently on the corners. Ah yes, there's the old oak, Big Rock, the path around the swamp. And over there, behind the haunted house, that must be the place. That pile of little diamonds must show where the treasure is hidden. That's not far from here! Let's go find it.

Only the stodgy and infirm can resist the lure of treasure. The Gold Rush, sunken treasure, the tomb of King Tutankhamen have captured the imaginations of countless seekers, old and young alike. Mention treasure to three- and four-year-olds and their ears perk up. Unruly gangs of nine- and ten-year-olds can become a captive and submissive audience if the promise of treasure is hinted at.

For me, hunting for treasure is one of the core metaphors for what education is all about. One of the objectives of schooling should be to engage students in searching for the meaning of life—the quest for the Holy Grail. When students get really enraptured in a topic and start to search for pieces of information, see the connections between different ideas, and then glimpse the big pattern, they're really engaged in a kind of treasure hunt. I see treasure hunts as embodying the best of what many progressive theorists refer to as "constructivist learning." Treasure hunts with elementary students provide a concrete illustration of the process of doing research and probing into the hidden recesses of a subject that happens in secondary school and in professional lives.

In the Upper Valley towns of New Hampshire and Vermont, educators have created an elegant, regional, place-based education treasure hunt that weaves together curriculum development, family recreation, and ecotourism. For their social studies and science curriculum, classroom teachers and students create treasure hunts to cultural and natural areas of significance—forgotten village centers, hilltop views, historic Shaker ritual sites, old-growth forests. It's integrated curriculum at its best—involving poetry writing, mapmaking, primary-source texts, field studies. When completed, they're all

collected into the Valley Quest guides that are used by historical societies, families, 4-H groups, and garden clubs to provide compelling treasure hunts. At the hiding place, questers find a secret box with a journal, educational information, and a unique rubber stamp and ink pad so you can gather an impression in your quest book. (See Chapter 7, "Valley Quest: Strengthening Community Through Educational Treasure Hunts," for a full description of this and other permanent treasure hunts.)

On a more everyday basis, I've seen treasure hunts used throughout the elementary grades to provide scaffolding for all the different curriculum areas. One kindergarten/first-grade teacher started the school year off with a pictorial treasure hunt that worked perfectly for all her nonreaders. After the first teacher-constructed hunt, the children started to create their own hunts, both inside the building and in the woods around the school. Treasure hunting expanded and became the theme or motif for the whole year in her classroom. Even when they weren't doing treasure hunts, the vocabulary of treasure hunting—finding clues, making maps, figuring out meanings, searching, uncovering hidden things—was the vocabulary they used when talking about problems in math and when learning to read. "I tried to make deciphering the clues attainable for everyone by including a picture clue on the back of each clue card as a fallback method if reading proved too difficult," she explained.

I've seen treasure hunts used in a fifth-grade mathematics curriculum where each clue led to a number problem on the schoolgrounds. In Keene, New Hampshire, the Robin Hood Forest treasure hunt was used as part of the environmental education curriculum for teaching map-reading skills in fourth grade. In Norwich, Vermont, an architectural clues treasure hunt was used in the fifth-grade social studies curriculum to introduce a unit on American history. And I've designed treasure hunts purely in books to teach library skills. One of my favorites was the Family Fun Day Pirate Treasure Hunt created for families with young children in Peterborough, New Hampshire. The hunt included finding snorkeling and excavating equipment to use for locating treasure that was actually in a chest sunk in about five feet of water about one hundred feet from shore. Very exciting. This was a true multigenerational event and is an excellent prototype for a school celebration.

To introduce a new state park to the people of southern New Hampshire about fifteen years ago, we created the Pisgah State Park treasure hunt. The clues, published in the local paper, required research in local libraries and historical societies, poring over old maps, and using natural history field guides. The treasure was a leather bag filled with fifty silver dollars. A treasure with real heft. After the event was completed, I received a letter from a sixty-year-old grandmother who said, "My husband and I traveled all over Pisgah trying to find answers to all the clues. We climbed the hills, explored the old village sites of Hardscrabble and Nash City, and enjoyed the solitude. We never found the real treasure, but we discovered that the real treasure was the beauty of this lost piece of New Hampshire, right out our back door."

That kind of sums it all up, doesn't it?

IN CONCLUSION

This chapter has been like the Family Fun Day Pirate Treasure Hunt I just described above. I've provided you with the tools to dig for your own treasure. The design principles are the tools; the treasure is the compelling education experiences you're going to design. And if you're really lucky, along the way some children will have transcendent experiences that you'll probably never know about. But what you will know is that your students, or your children, have had indelible experiences of true immersion in the natural world. And as my twenty-year-old daughter recently wrote in a letter to me: "This connection to the earth, which is everywhere and always nurturing, is one of the greatest gifts I have ever received; it allows me to feel at home anywhere I can plant my feet in the soil and hug the trees and helps me to find solitude and peace within myself and the world around me."

Sounds like the Holy Grail to me.

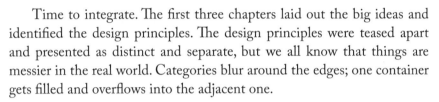

Introduction to Chapters 4–11:
The Rest of the Stories

Time to integrate. The first three chapters laid out the big ideas and identified the design principles. The design principles were teased apart and presented as distinct and separate, but we all know that things are messier in the real world. Categories blur around the edges; one container gets filled and overflows into the adjacent one.

The following essays—Chapters 4 through 11—were written over the past ten years and have appeared in a variety of books and magazines. But they're all tied together by these design principle strands. In some essays, I'm railing against children's lives lived indoors and advocating for more fresh air and real adventure. In other essays, I'm describing great examples of vibrant programs or provocative curricula. But in each case, the design principles serve as the core elements that inspire the educators to immerse students in the natural world. The results are both a love of the natural world and curriculum that wholeheartedly meets the standards and goes way beyond.

I've provided each essay with a prelude that identifies some of the design principles at work. You'll notice that there are often two or three principles woven together. Icons on the first page of each of these chapters indicate which design principles are applied in that chapter. There are fewer examples of Special Places because many of these are identified in my previous book on this topic. And you'll probably see elements of some of the principles that I haven't identified. Even better, I hope that you'll realize that some of your programs have been successful because you unknowingly were using some of the design principles. If that's the case, let me know about them.

For instance, I loved recently finding out about the Midsummer's Eve celebration at the Minnetrista Cultural Center in Muncie, Indiana. Here,

a local dancer trains local children to each develop a flower fairy persona. Each child chooses a flower, learns its attributes, and then develops a movement repertoire based on the flower's attributes. The child and teacher also develop a dance outfit based on the appearance of the flower. For two or three nights around the summer solstice, the center invites the community to come stroll the brick pathways through the preserved Ball Estate Victorian gardens. Frolicking flower fairies haunt candlelit pathways amidst the azaleas, lilies, and periwinkle. What a wonderful illustration of using the Fantasy and Imagination design principle to engage children in botanical learning.

Because of these fairy experiences, I suspect that these children are more likely to grow into adults who want to garden. Perhaps magic is the link between love and knowledge.

DESIGN PRINCIPLES ILLUSTRATED THROUGHOUT THE BOOK

	Adventure	Fantasy and Imagination	Animal Allies	Maps and Paths	Special Places	Small Worlds	Hunting and Gathering
Chapter 1 *Replacing Contempt with Love*				♦		♦	
Chapter 2 *"Appareled in Celestial Light"*	♦	♦					
Chapter 3 *Children and Nature Design Principles*	♦	♦	♦	♦	♦	♦	♦
Chapter 4 *Take Back the Afternoon*	♦		♦		♦		
Chapter 5 *Mapping McCabe*				♦			♦
Chapter 6 *Authentic Curriculum*	♦	♦	♦			♦	
Chapter 7 *Valley Quest*				♦			♦
Chapter 8 *The Sky Above, the Internet Below*	♦						
Chapter 9 *Island Play*	♦	♦		♦			♦
Chapter 10 *Place-Based Education in Guilford, Vermont*	♦	♦		♦		♦	♦
Chapter 11 *Global Climate Change Meets Ecophobia*						♦	
Epilogue: *Ancient Greece in Vermont*		♦					

CHAPTER 4
TAKE BACK THE AFTERNOON

Prelude

Although written a decade ago, this essay is even more relevant today. It originally appeared in an issue of the Massachusetts Audubon Society's Sanctuary *magazine dedicated to the theme "The Loss of Real Play." It turned out to be the most requested back issue ever, because parents were really concerned about this change they were noticing in their children's lives. And as computer software gets more interactive and sophisticated, there's a danger that children will be further seduced away from the natural world. Since then, Richard Louv's book* Last Child in the Woods *has brought this concern to a national level, and the bandwagon that I advocate for in the last paragraph has been created.*

The real world can be just as compelling as the computer world if we use the design principles to construct outdoor experiences. Alice McLerra's book Roxaboxen *is a good example of a Special Places world created by children in the 1930s. The children in this essay bemoan not being able to play like this, but an increasing number of schools are recognizing the character-building and academic values of schoolyard forts. Over the past year, the principal and teachers at the Greenfield, New Hampshire, Elementary School have encouraged and supported a fort culture on the woodsy edge of their schoolyard with great success. The interactivity in these fort villages is equally compelling as the virtual simulations of Club Penguin or Second Life.*

Instead of sedentary computerism, I advocate for the preservation of many traditional childhood Adventure activities here. Bending birches, playing Capture the Flag, and good old-fashioned pond hockey are the kind of afternoon activities we still need to cultivate in this age of wall-to-wall organized sports.

Finally, I describe a classroom project that applies the Animal Allies principle in an unconventional way. Though we usually think of children connecting with

ADVENTURE
◆

ANIMAL
ALLIES
◆

SPECIAL
PLACES
◆

either cute and cuddly animals (kittens, lambs, baby birds) or charismatic megafauna (jaguars, musk ox, wolves), the fourth graders described here become ardent protectors of a species of California freshwater shrimp, about as uncuddly and uncharismatic an animal as you can find. But because it's in their backyard and it needs their help, they become its ally.

Have you seen the advertisements? The four-year-old sits propped on a couple of pillows or telephone books gazing into the computer. She is bathed in soft, multi-colored light while the rest of the room is in shadow. The light suggests alpenglow, the radiant magenta softness that high peaks catch from the setting sun while the rest of the landscape is subdued in twilight. The computer glow is supposed to be subtly beautiful; this is a moment of quiet reverence and thoughtful contemplation. The computer industry has discovered a new market—preschool-age children.

I recently read a quote from a prominent business magazine that suggested that by the age of six, a child's buying habits can be fully determined for the rest of his or her life. Therefore, if marketers can cultivate a predisposition to consumerism at an early age, they can lock children into being permanent targets of manufactured goods for the rest of their lives. If they can get kids hooked on computers and software at an early age, then manufacturers can be assured of sixty years of lifelong technoconsuming. It is just like Louisiana Pacific's practice of planting seedlings to harvest after four decades of growth, and it may be producing the same kind of monotonous monoculture in our children's minds.

A founder of a small school in northern California described his concerns about the computer issue to me. All the parents sending their children to the school had a deep ecological consciousness and were very progressive. But as soon as their children were in first grade they wanted to know, "When is the school going to get computers?" They couldn't really articulate why they thought computers were important for young children, but they were anxious to have their kids jump on the bandwagon so they wouldn't get left behind.

Capitalizing on these latent fears and parental concerns, the advertising hook is, If you love your child, buy her a computer! But does the computer really make your preschooler smarter, happier, and healthier? Or does it numb her brain and make her just another contributor to the globalization of a consumer-oriented, ecologically destructive culture?

Regrettably, it is not simply black and white. Rather, to paraphrase Judy Collins, "Something's lost and something's gained in computer use every day." When children in and out of school are using computers, they are *not doing* something else. If we understand what they are not doing as well as what they are doing, we will be in a better position to decide what place computers should have in children's lives.

I got a perspective on the after-school situation from talking with an environmental educator who works with a group of fourth graders in our small city of Keene, New Hampshire, which is surrounded by parks and woods. This past spring the educator read the children Alice McLerra's *Roxaboxen*, a book about children creating a fantasy town while growing up in the American West in the 1930s. It is a simple portrait of independent imaginative play. "Oh, those children are so lucky. I wish we could do that," was the children's response. The teacher was surprised. She had assumed the children would easily identify with the children in the story, so she asked them what they did after school. Of the sixteen children in the class, two of the children were not allowed to go outside, four said they watched TV or talked on the phone, six went to the recreation center to play video games, and four played outside. If this is a representative sample, then only 25 percent of nine-year-old children in our safe, all-American city are out playing in the neighborhood after school.

This resonates eerily with a child's comment collected by Richard Louv in research for his book *Childhood's Future*. When Louv asked a group of fourth graders whether they liked to play indoors or outdoors better, one fourth grader responded, "I like to play indoors better 'cause that's where the electrical outlets are" (1991). I do not have to tell you *what* they are playing inside, do I?

This erosion of childhood concerns me. Computers seem like a river in flood, washing away the soil that roots children to the natural world. Elementary-age children, now more than ever, need opportunities to be in their bodies in the world—jump roping, bicycling, stream-hopping, and fort-building. It's in this engagement between the limbs of the body and the bones of the earth where true balance and centeredness emerge.

But as computer recreation bulldozes a swath across young minds, whole species of New England childhood pastimes are becoming extinct. When, for instance, was the last time you saw a child bending birches? It used to be a staple of farm childhoods, mostly in the spring, when the sap rising in white birches made them most elastic. Robert Frost was proud of being a "swinger of birches," and he realized the skills inherent in the refinement of the practice. A boy chooses a field-edge birch with just a few branches, not too skinny, not too fat, and shinnies up the tree...

❖   ❖   ❖

He learned all there was

To learn about not launching out too soon

And so not carrying the tree away

Clear to the ground. He always kept his poise

To the top branches, climbing carefully

With the same pains you use to fill a cup

Up to the brim, and even above the brim.

Then he flung outward, feet first, with a swish,

Kicking his way down through the air to the ground.

(1916)

❖   ❖   ❖

In tuning the body to the birch, the child sensed the literal interdependence between himself and the natural world. He felt the analogy between the flexibility of the trunk and the comfortable suppleness of his own body. And he knew, deep in his heart, that he was responsible—he measured the risk and designed the task. When the software's on the screen, someone else is in charge. And the analogy that reigns is mind as computer, not person as living organism.

Childhood games have gone the same way; they've become mechanized and consumerized. Whatever happened to neighborhood-wide Capture the Flag and Kick the Can? I lived for those twilight evenings of scheming and sneaking and finding yourself nose to nose with a toad but having to contain your giggles so you wouldn't get caught in enemy territory. Hockey's a great example of the adulteration of childhood. Nowadays it's icetime at 4:30 in the morning, a fortune spent on gear, weekends spent driving for hours, and five-dollar rewards offered to kids who'll take down the high scorer on the other team. The landscape is industrial ice, pallor-inducing stadium lights, and Zamboni fumes. Charles McGrath, in a recent *Outside* magazine article, sings the praises of pond hockey, a game that was more like improvisational jazz than prerecorded keyboard jingles.

Some of that pastoral quality still lingered even when I was growing up, outside Boston, in the fifties and early sixties. I may be one of the last generation of Boston schoolkids who never skated on artificial ice until I started playing hockey in high school. All through grammar school I played on reservoirs and frozen playgrounds and ponds; we would sometimes trek for hours from one spot to another, our feet and fingers numb, in search of better ice—a kind of wintry grail, always shimmering just a littler farther on. (1997)

In our rush to prematurely instill competitive values, we've diminished the experience. McGrath speculates that "In teaching kids from a very early age all the systems of hockey—where to line up, where to sit on the bench, where to be on a three on two—we may have deprived them of some of the joy that comes from just playing, from fooling around and figuring things out on your own" (1997). And pond hockey connects you with the weather, lets you appreciate the silver lining of snow followed by rain, and challenges you to understand the physics of ice.

Regardless of whether it's indoor or outdoor hockey, however, I suspect that either is more valuable than the software version now available on CD. Computers invite children to be inside, in their heads, sedentary and unconnected to people and animals and trees. We have a computer at home, and every now and then, especially in the winter, the kids will go on a little computer jag. Nowadays they're really into Quest for Glory. But after school and before supper in April and May, they disappear outside as soon as they get home. They ride bikes, make forts, and pretend they are lost children, smell the wet dog trilliums, play baseball, knock on neighbors' doors and hide in the bushes. They arrive back for dinner with flushed cheeks and muddy pants and I feel completely happy and grateful for living in a safe neighborhood with other parents who believe in the simple joys of fresh air and friendship. Everyone sleeps better when afternoons are filled with recreation rather than Reader Rabbit.

Computer use in school may be something of a different story. My children regularly comment that computer class is one of their favorite things in school. The interactivity and dynamic immediacy of good software *is* appealing. Getting immersed in a good computer game like Myst is like getting engrossed in a good book. The problem-solving, chronology-deciphering and mapmaking are compelling and, to me, invite the development of thinking skills. And watch kids at work on Sim-City or the Oregon Trail. Despite the inherent limitations and hidden values of the software designers,

the immediate feedback on the decisions you make and the compression of time allow children a kind of time-lapse photography insight into historical processes.

The message here is that good software is much more dynamic and interactive than most of the rest of the stuff that goes on in school. Working on the computer gives you a sense of playing with another thoughtful, playful, and complex mind. Sitting at your desk and taking dictation or listening to a lecture makes you feel like a drone. Be honest with yourself. Would you rather do pages 37 to 39 in the language arts workbook or telecommunicate with students in New Orleans and correct each other's spelling sentences this week?

This does not mean, however, that we should cave in to demands for more and more computers in schools. Instead, we need to focus on creating learning environments and educational challenges that are equally engaging, interactive, and sophisticated as good software. Like the bully who threatens to take over the classroom, the computer needs to be put in its place. The old Sufi saying, "If you only have a hammer, everything looks like a nail," has relevance here. Technology enthusiasts want us to believe that *all* educational problems are nails and that we can solve them by giving everyone a computer hammer. But cooperative learning, apprenticeships, real science, social-action projects, and community-based environmental education are equally important tools in creating educational reform.

Laurette Rogers understands the potency of project-based learning and the appropriate role of the computer in the process. As a fourth-grade teacher in San Anselmo, California, she was studying endangered species with her class. But her students got frustrated with passive learning about the problem; instead, they wanted to do something about it. The children decided that since the California freshwater shrimp was both in their backyard *and* endangered, they would initiate a campaign to preserve shrimp habitat. A one-month science unit blossomed into a four-year project that is still under way. Laurette reports that

> the students work in committees and basically learn every aspect of running a nonprofit organization. Our main activities are educating the public about the plight of the endangered species and also habitat rehabilitation. We work with ranchers, planting native plants, getting funding for fencing and so on... It is community building because it breaks down the walls of the classroom and has students working with community members, so the classroom really becomes a network that builds community. (1996)

Since the project requires communication, the students are responsible for writing and producing a newsletter that requires using page design software. In addition, they use the Internet to research habitat restoration techniques used in other projects. But they are also using water test kits, microscopes, field guides, shovels, and dip nets. And consensus building, debating, money management, and testifying at public hearings are equally important as learning word-processing on the classroom computer.

The point here is that computers should follow, not lead. Dynamic, real-life engagements that build skills, self-confidence, and a sense of purpose in life are the motivating force of education. The computer has a role to play in this drama, but it should be a supporting cast member, not the star. Right now, the computer is too much of a prima donna, attracting attention away from the rest of the players and the technical crew. And if an increasing percentage of the school budget is spent on computers, then not enough will be spent on pianos, art materials, laboratory equipment, land acquisition for the nature center, bilingual education specialists, and a new sound system for the theater.

Like television, computers encourage our children to become couch potatoes. The sophisticated processes of critical thinking, problem-solving, and kinesthetic coordination appropriately mature out of children's interaction with concrete materials, caring adults, and thoughtfully managed groups of peers. Luring children into the world of pure information and electronic images alienates them from experience and disembodies their learning. But in concert with active learning, computers can enhance the educational experience. In all things, moderation.

I will never forget sitting next to Joseph Chilton Pearce, the noted author of *The Crack in the Cosmic Egg* and *Magical Child*, at a presentation about educational software. Storybook Weaver, an integrated graphics and word-processing program for children, was on display. To make a picture you choose from a variety of landscapes—skies, mountains, rivers, yards—and then you choose people, animals, buildings, and the like to fill out the image. It's all clip art. Then you can add text to the pictures and with a bunch of these you create a story. Unfamiliar with this kind of software, Joe was taken aback. As he watched the presenter flip through a variety of prefab landscapes, his eyes filled with tears. "This isn't imagination or creativity, it's just…" and he was overcome with sadness. Drawing pictures and making up stories is something that most children take to with little prompting. If the software does it for them, are we stealing away the image-making capacity from children? Does Storybook Weaver just encourage children to become consumers of externally produced images?

Let us make it acceptable for parents and teachers to Just Say No to significant amounts of television and computers until children enter adolescence. Childhood is

short enough; there is no need to hasten its demise with exposure to soul-depleting electronic media. In my household, we figure it is a good idea to immunize our children against the onslaught of mass culture by allowing them three or four hours of combined television or computer use per week. This avoids the forbidden-fruit effect and gives us good material for dinnertime conversations. And in place of electronic media, let us work for dynamic classrooms and safe neighborhoods. I say we start a new movement called Take Back the Afternoon that advocates for good, old-fashioned real play, at least a couple of days a week. Perhaps we can create our own bandwagon.

CHAPTER 5
MAPPING MCCABE
Connecting Curriculum and Community

by David Sobel and Susie Spikol

Prelude

This short essay just hints at the bigger world of place-based education that has emerged in the last decade. Recognizing the life-dulling and disconnecting effect that the No Child Left Behind testing frenzy has had on teachers and students, some school leaders have a better idea. They're trying to increase academic achievement through grounding the curriculum in real landscapes and community issues. The result is better test scores, more community vitality, increased stewardship behavior, and a healthier environment.

Mapping McCabe was just one of the early place-based projects at the Great Brook Middle School in Antrim, New Hampshire. Students have recently mapped town conservation land, designed and created outdoor classrooms, and helped students with disabilities learn to ski at Mt. Sunapee. To map the McCabe Forest, land owned by a statewide conservation organization, students, teachers, and naturalists did a number of recurrent walking field trips to study the mammals, birds, and flora. These trips were organized with the Hunting and Gathering design principle in mind. To understand what animals lived in McCabe, the students followed tracks, read signs, collected scat, and gathered plant materials for classroom identification. In true exploratory fashion, they never knew what they'd find.

Because this project had a cartographic outcome, it also illustrates the Maps and Paths principle. Each class of fifth-grade students worked with a Harris Center naturalist, their classroom teacher, and the art teacher to create elegant, illustrated maps of the mammals, birds, and trees of the forest. Each student chose one species to focus on (a fox, or a grouse, or a white pine, for instance), mapped the places where that organism lived within McCabe, then drew, wrote

**MAPS &
PATHS**
◆

**HUNTING &
GATHERING**
◆

poetry, and described the natural history of that organism. All the individual contributions were woven together by the art teacher into coherent, texturized four-by-six-foot maps— many of which still grace our graduate school halls today. They are a synthesis of artistry, solid academic learning, and rootedness. And they are just as persuasive at demonstrating school success as high test scores.

INTO THE WILD

It is a perfect day for tracking. A couple of inches of new-fallen snow hides the thick icy mess of the winter of '98–'99. A group of Great Brook Middle School fifth graders stands huddled together with hats pulled down and scarves wrapped tight, just their eyes peeking out, bright and excited. We have come to the Forest Society's McCabe Forest in Antrim, a ten-minute walk from the school, to track and map the wild creatures who call this land their home. Armed with rulers, field guides, and inquisitiveness, we trek off in search of paw prints, scat, and stories to be unraveled.

It doesn't take long to find our first track. On the edge of the huge field, a boy with sharp eyes discovers a series of prints that look like a small child's hand. We gather around the tracks, careful not to step on them, and like detectives, students begin the task of collecting evidence. Together we share our data, confirming measurements and comparing them to the field guides. Raccoon is our lead suspect. The measurements match perfectly and as we follow the tracks they lead right to the compost pile, confirming an old tracker saying, "When in doubt, follow it out."

This tracking trip was the first of several as this class worked on mapping the mammals of McCabe Forest. Each time we visited the forest, students with eyes as sharp as hawks uncovered evidence of McCabe's furry inhabitants. From the small tunnels unearthed by moles to the river otter's mussel middens, the wildlife secrets slowly unfolded before our searching eyes.

Two other fifth-grade classes focused their maps and inventories on the birdlife and flora of the forest. These fifth graders became seekers of all that flew, grew, scurried, and scampered as they journeyed through winter and spring, watching McCabe's landscape change from winter's white to spring's mud to early summer's green explosion.

Their cartographic explorations all came together in the elegant maps of McCabe's natural resources that are now displayed at the Forest Society's headquarters.

GROUNDING THE CURRICULUM

Mapping McCabe is just one of many projects that have emerged out of the Community-based School Environmental Education project (CO-SEED), a cooperative project involving Great Brook, the Antrim community, the Harris Center, and Antioch University New England. Two other partnerships with the new Rivendell Interstate School District and Hulbert Outdoors Center and with the Gorham, New Hampshire, schools, Trail Master, and the Appalachian Mountain Club are also under way.

The common theme in these efforts is our desire to bring the environment and the community into the core of the curriculum. For too long, we feel, environmental education had been like art, a tassel on the edge of the school fabric, not the warp. Our objective is to make ecological literacy a serious part of the school philosophy. Through grounding the curriculum in local places, we make learning more meaningful and we increase student achievement.

In each community, the environments we focus on radiate outward from the school like ever-larger Russian nesting dolls. In the schools, we are setting up recycling programs and creating classroom and kitchen composting systems. On the Great Brook schoolgrounds, sixth-grade teacher Kitty Swan had her students design an outdoor classroom. In the Antrim community, fifth- and sixth-grade teachers Barbara Black and Letitia Rice facilitated a yearlong project in conjunction with the Antrim Conservation Committee to revitalize downtown Memorial Park. Students mapped the park, identified existing flora, researched native flora, came up with landscape design proposals, made presentations to town committees, and, finally, implemented the planting scheme in the late spring.

The McCabe Forest serves as the wild edge for the whole system. McCabe is the accessible wilderness—close enough to walk to, but big enough to get lost in. Its 136 acres harbor mixed hardwood forests, open meadows, rocky brooks, spacious pine groves, and floodplain oxbows. Sixth graders can camp here and feel like they're really away from it all, but still make it to an evening soccer game.

THE STREAM RUNS THROUGH IT

We stand in the flowing waters of No-Name Stream in Antrim's McCabe Forest. Our feet rest on the slippery cobble and the brook's current tugs at us. Today, it is the caddis-fly larva that has captivated us. These distinctive invertebrates construct shelters out of a variety of small objects gathered from the streambed and fastened together with a gluelike spit or silk. Each type of case reveals a different species of caddis fly. There are cases built from last year's leaves, rough twigs, slender pine needles, and small shimmering pebbles.

As we observe these creatures, I look around at my crew of collectors and am struck by a strange comparison, an interspecies metaphor. Like the caddis fly, we build who we are by what is around us and where we have come from. This seems particularly true for middle school students as they begin their slow and often difficult transition from childhood to adulthood. They construct their portable self, and although they will emerge as their own adult, their school and community experiences can shape the home that will always be a part of them. We want those cases to be constructed of New Hampshire leaves and pebbles of community service rather than shreds of MTV and Tommy Hilfiger.

I watch as each child gently lowers the young caddis fly back into the stream's grasp. I cannot help but feel a fluid kinship. Here I am with tomorrow's leaders, standing in the cool spring water, watching as they bid good-bye to their little larvae. I hear soft voices whispering to the flies: "Good-bye, little one," "Don't get eaten," and "Grow into a great fly."

Yes, all good words of advice. I whisper too. The stream of life washes over our ankles and imparts the sustaining strength of granite.

CHAPTER 6
AUTHENTIC CURRICULUM

Prelude

Written more than ten years ago, this essay captures some of my emergent thinking about children and nature design principles. I've updated some of the language to make it current, but as with many of the older essays in this book, their relevance has been heightened by recent education-reform initiatives.

It's useful, I hope, to think of the children and nature design principles as "authentic"; that is, as attempting to identify deep, recurrent longings in children, because doing so can lead you to develop activities and curriculum that will authentically captivate children. Though lots of bases are covered in this essay, four design principles are clearly illustrated. The story "Let the Floodwaters Go," in the section "A Living, Breathing Example," illustrates a curriculum inspired by Small Worlds. To this day, it's hard for me to resist damming little streams on the beach; providing an outlet for the hidden engineer in all of us is a sure way to get students involved.

The Becoming Birds activity was another one of those serendipitous curriculum ideas, based on the Animal Allies principle, that took wing. As curriculum planners, we started from the premise that children need to become animals before they can learn about them or save them. By honoring the becoming of birds, students got seriously interested in learning about them. My contention is that their growth in content knowledge was much greater because we honored the authentic process of learning from the inside out.

The Smuggling Gold literature study is a quiet example of using Adventure in the classroom. Yes, adventure often means big challenges—following streams, trying out ropes courses, caving—but it can also mean instigating a secret plot right within the walls of the school. Through simulating the Norwegian children's smuggling of gold past Nazi guards in WWII, these fifth-grade students had a rich text-to-self experience that provoked both emotional and cognitive

ADVENTURE
◆

FANTASY &
IMAGINATION
◆

ANIMAL
ALLIES
◆

SMALL
WORLDS
◆

understanding of children's experience of war. The simulated quality of adventures places this activity in the Fantasy and Imagination design principle as well.

THE BIRD IN THE WINDOW

The emphasis on high-stakes testing and curricular standardization caused by the No Child Left Behind movement over the past five years has been discouraging. Discouraging because I watched the national curriculum developments in England in the 1990s and heard teachers describe the things that were lost as a result. Discouraging because the standards movement often threatens many beneficial developments that have emerged in the name of site-based management, place-based education, and teacher ownership of the curriculum here in the United States

The situation in England is particularly disheartening because, to my mind, many British teachers and small primary schools have carried the banner of what I want to call *authentic curriculum* since the 1960s. Authentic curriculum refers to curriculum that springs forth from the genuine, unmediated individual and developmental fascinations of children and teachers. In a talk to a group of British teachers in 1969, educational philosopher David Hawkins described one source of authentic curriculum, saying,

> *Everyone knows that the best times in teaching have always been the consequences of some little accident that happened to direct attention in some new way, to revitalize an old interest which has died out or to create a brand new interest that you hadn't had any notion about how to introduce. Suddenly there it is. The bird flies in the window and that's the miracle you needed.* (1973)

British teachers have become masters at dealing with the "bird in the window." Responsive to the shell that Fiona brings in after holidays, or to the news story that connects with yesterday's classroom event, or to just the right book that fits with Roger and Ben's construction in the block area, British teachers have created and shaped curriculum out of the unique chemistry of the individuals and events in their classrooms. As the national curriculum implementation has proceeded in England, it is disappointing to hear teachers comment that these special, idiosyncratic projects and pursuits are gradually being elbowed aside or not allowed to grow and flourish because of the pressure to cover all the mandated material. "There's just no *time* nowadays," they complain.

This righteous and compelling demand for curricular comprehensiveness and consistency extirpates local color and character in classrooms. It's like the homogenization of the American commercial landscape by fast-food restaurants or the decimation of traditional cultural practices with the arrival of television and a market economy.

I have always heard that you can walk into any second-grade classroom in France—whether in Paris or Lyon or Marseille—and the children will be working on the same pages in the workbook. This may seem like the fulfillment of the national curriculum dream. To me, it's a nightmare. Rather, I have always said that a diagnostic feature of a good classroom is being able to walk in and see something happening that you've never seen before. The intersection of twenty children's concerns and interests, the teacher's passion, the cultural milieu, and the prescribed curriculum in all its permutations and combinations should generate some new species of curricular flowers. Maybe not every day, but at least once every few months. If this isn't happening, the magic and mystery of learning, of knowledge unfolding, isn't present. Its preservation is as important as the protection of rain forests in Costa Rica or dwarf wedge mussels in southern New Hampshire.

FROM THE INSIDE OUT

Is *authentic curriculum* a new idea? Do we really need a new term to describe something that's been around for a long time? Certainly, many competing terms exist that seem to describe the same approaches. There's *integrated curriculum, developmentally appropriate curriculum*, thematic or *project-centered curriculum*, as well as *informal education* and that old bugaboo, *open education*. Authentic curriculum certainly overlaps with all of these, but it is not synonymous with any of them.

The term *authentic curriculum* emerged out of our work in the Department of Education at Antioch University New England. In preparing comments in summer 1989 for our annual first community meeting with new students in the Integrated Day program, I realized I wanted to talk, in specific terms, about what the faculty believed in. I wanted to go beyond the grand, eloquent ringing phrases about honoring individual development *and* social responsibility or about the symbiotic *I-Thou-It* relationship between the child, the teacher, and the curriculum. I wanted to model particularity by describing actual examples of good curricular practice in classrooms. The examples all had an insistent, self-affirming quality about them—like the

seemingly delicate plant that pushes its way through asphalt—a quality that origi-
nates down deep, and then moves, indomitably, up and out.

My former wife, an expressive-arts therapist, was at that time involved in a new
form of choreography and therapy. She described it as "movement from the inside out,"
where the individual meditates, or quiets herself, and allows movement to emerge. In
contrast to head-down movement—thinking about the movement and then instruct-
ing the body to perform—the idea was to eliminate the mind as source and let the
body stir movement within. The mind became active only after the movement session, looking at the movement patterns and images and reflecting on their significance.
This methodology is described as *authentic movement*. I realized it conveyed the same
dynamic principle that I wanted to convey about curriculum.

Because I had prepared my comments the night before the meeting, I was not
able to share my thinking with my colleagues. Instead, after I introduced the term
and shared my examples, I asked other education faculty if they had similar illustrative examples. Without hesitation, everyone shared poignant portraits of similar kinds
of classroom work, some of which I share here. Since coined, *authentic curriculum* has
started to stand on its own. It has carved out a niche in our semantic universe and we
are constantly on the lookout for living and breathing examples of authentic curriculum. This sense of *rightness* or *fittingness* that we feel supports our conviction that we
are describing a distinct species of classroom practice. Certainly, it's been seen before,
but since it looks like other similar species and occurs infrequently, it's never been taxo-
nomically differentiated. Before it falls before the chain saws of curriculum reform, I
want to try to qualify and describe it.

The term *authentic curriculum* differs from the notion of *authentic assessment*. The
terms bear much in common, but I think it's important to distinguish between the
quality of authenticity as implied by the advocates of authentic assessment and the
quality of authenticity in curriculum as we have described it in the education department at Antioch New England.

What's taught in schools is often different from what's assessed. Hence, the objective of authentic assessment is to bridge this discrepancy by bringing the assessment in
line with the true goals of the curriculum, or to bring internal consistency or coherence
to the curriculum/assessment cycle. But the goals of the curriculum *and* the assessment are generally determined by administration and teachers and reside mostly in the
objective external world, apart from the inner lives of children.

Authentic curriculum, on the other hand, refers more to the process of movement from the inside out, taking curriculum impulses from the inside of the child

and bringing them out into the light of day, in the classroom. It implies a necessary connection between the subjective, inner lives of children and the objective, external world of schooling. Froebel, the nineteenth-century creator of the kindergarten, suggested an analogous pedagogical dynamic when he said, "For the purpose of teaching and instruction is to bring ever more out of man rather than to put more and more into him" (Froebel 1970).

A LIVING, BREATHING EXAMPLE

Time to get specific. The following narrative is adapted from a journal entry written when I was teaching a group of first graders at The Harrisville School in Harrisville, New Hampshire. It is useful here as a springboard for a discussion of the salient attributes of authentic curriculum.

Let the Floodwaters Go, 28 April 1973

The ever-present spring drizzle had stopped just a few minutes before, so I decided to let the children go outside for recess. Granted, they were going to get their feet wet, but it had been raining for too many days to keep them inside again. The air was beginning to freshen, the new leaves glistened and the nerve-wracking black flies were still holed up enough to make it a beautiful, though gray, morning. Brian and Chip gravitated to the waterworks area and began to create two dams, one above the other. This area is created where a small drainpipe empties out from underground onto a muddy hillside, and a child-sized rivulet courses down the hill, begging to be shaped. Regularly, two or three boys would play in this area, but soon a dozen different boys had converged and a massive project began to take form.

The cooperation was admirable. Somehow, all the boys seemed to parcel themselves out into specific roles. Some tended the upper dam, some the lower one. There were channelizers, and two boys in charge of controlling the flow of water from the pipe. Then there were the mud and clay collectors preparing the materials for the dam tenders. It suggested many images of beavers and bees. The fascinating aspect was that no one was in charge. There were many conflicting ideas, lots of arguments about whether to heighten this dam, deepen this pool, when to let the water out of the pipe, but they were all worked out without a hitch. Everyone was caught up in the building, the mud and the clay, the flow of the water, the necessity to keep the dam strong. Frequently someone would warn, "Ten minutes till the flood!"

I let things go way past the end of recess, not wanting to intercede, but then finally told them that they'd have to bring things to an end. The consensus was to break down the dams. "Let the floodwaters go! Let the floodwaters go!" they chanted spontaneously. The dams were burst one after the other and the water poured down the hillside to everyone's great delight. I reminded everyone to wash, remove his muddy shoes, and come to the rug for discussion. Chip, who had been a clay preparer, wanted to save some of the clay, so we set it aside to see what would happen to it.

My initial plan for discussion was to draw a large, collective map of the whole project. I thought we would talk about trapping the water, how the water got from one place to another, other ways of making the system bigger, adding more channels, more dams, and so on. I was interested to see how much they could move from their kinesthetic involvement in the mud and water to a two-dimensional representation. After they created the map, I planned to send them back to change the dam system the next day.

I started by asking some questions about the source of the water, calling only on those with raised hands in order to organize their enthusiasm. When I asked about how they made the water run faster, Peter explained, "By holding it back by damming it." This led us into talking about dam construction. It seemed, Brian summarized, the significant problem with the dams was that if you didn't keep repairing them, "the water would seep through little holes in the bottom of the dam, holes you can't see, and then the holes get bigger and more water comes through." He explained with a lot of gestures, one hand showing the dam and wiggling fingers on the other hand showing the trickling water.

About this point, I abandoned the map idea and started asking about the differences between clay and mud as building materials, a difference they had introduced. Chip said, "Clay is better. It's stickier and it holds together more." I pulled out Chip's clay, and Mary, my assistant, went to get some potting soil. I thought we'd see about the differences between clay and dirt. I made a ball of clay and a ball of mud and asked the children what would happen if I put my finger in them both. Most agreed I would make a hole in both. When I stuck my finger in the clay one, it stayed together, whereas the dirt one fell apart. But at their urging, I made the dirt one wetter and after two more trials the dirt/mud ball stayed together too. "Is clay just wet dirt?" I queried. I then made another ball of each and put them in water and we watched the dirt one disintegrate while the clay one held together. "Are clay and dirt different other than just being wetter or drier than each other?" We set aside a ball of clay and a ball of mud to see what happened, and since we'd been at this for close to a half hour, we broke for lunch.

During the next two weeks we went off in a variety of directions. Some of the boys returned to the waterworks area and continued to build new structures, modify their dam-building techniques, and add more technology. One of the morning options became doing experiments with clay and mud to see which material was stronger. I showed one group how to make miniature bricks; they modified the procedure, made a lot of them, and then started building miniature houses with the bricks. Later on, this branched off into building structures with stones and concrete. From the brick-building activities we got into a series of discussions about the best way to build tall walls with building blocks. We built one wall with the blocks stacked on top of each other and another wall with the blocks overlapping each other. We then devised a way to standardize a sideways glancing blow to see which wall was stronger. The lessons from these discussions got applied to both their constructions with the unit blocks and in a bridge that they built out of the large blocks that spanned the hallway and connected two rooms together.

Another group became involved in modeling with the clay that we collected from the clay deposits outside. One morning, discussion focused on the differences between the potter's clay that we had in the school and the natural clay we found outside. Michael's parents, both professional potters, came and did some hand-building activities with these children.

That one vibrant damming experience and the discussion that followed resonated throughout the curriculum for the rest of the school year.

DEFINING THE ECOLOGY OF AUTHENTIC CURRICULUM

In my four years of working with children at The Harrisville School, there were no more than a dozen of these truly captivating involvements that turned into potent curriculum. The rest of the time we all went about the business of good education, holding to the daily rhythms, doing reading, writing, math, and theme work while we prepared and tried to lay the groundwork for the outbreak of authentic curriculum. David Hawkins says, "We all know that we can't succeed at it all the time or sometimes not even very often but we all also know that when it does happen it's worth a great deal because in fact far more is learned under those conditions than under conditions of routine presentation of subject matter" (1973).

What are some of the sources, the spawning grounds, of authentic curriculum? Many are embedded in the dam-building account. I will first try to isolate them and then describe them in greater depth with diverse examples.

PLAY

Children's play is often the fertile soil in which authentic curriculum takes root. If there are no times and places for children to play—and this applies throughout the elementary years—it will be very difficult for curricular impulses to emerge. Anticipating that the children were going to get very wet and muddy, it would have been reasonable for me to forbid their waterplay and attenuate the whole activity. Or, sensing the possibilities, I could have interceded early on and directed it toward my own ends. By staying out of it, a wave of energy emerged that sustained the children's involvement.

INDIVIDUAL FASCINATION

Although the waterworks example doesn't illustrate this in a striking fashion, individual fascination is often a crucial starting point. Authentic curriculum often emerges out of just one child's deep, persistent interest and fascination with something. It's like the dog that won't let go of the bone. In this case, Chip was one of the instigators. He could always be counted on to immerse himself in messy, shapeable projects, but his role in this capacity was fleeting on this occasion. Sometimes, one child labors on by himself for a long time before things start to snowball.

GROUP CHEMISTRY

The group that got involved in the waterworks project was in no way a happy, cooperative group. Squabbles and fights were regular occurrences. They often wanted nothing to do with each other. But the spontaneous colleagueship and cooperation that emerged during this activity was a striking example of the kind of rapture that characterizes curriculum at its best. It's similar to the spell that good storytellers are able to cast over an audience. Each child involved is buoyed up by each other child's involvement. My recognition that they were all riding this same wave of momentum was the reason I relaxed the recess boundaries and let it flow as long as seemed possible.

SERENDIPITY

Although sensitive teachers are able to set the stage for authentic curriculum, it often emerges out of the blue. Water issued forth from the drainpipe only when there was lots of groundwater. Our appearance on the playground soon after it had been raining for many days meant there was an unusually good flow of water that day. Had we skipped going out that day, the whole sequence of events might never have happened. The whimsical nature of when the curriculum muse will appear makes it hard to always stick to lesson plans.

TEACHER CAPITALIZATION

It would have been easy for me to either ignore the whole activity when we went back inside or to persist with my mapping idea. The first alternative would have squandered the rich curricular potential and the second would have very possibly squashed their interest. In providing the opportunity for them to share their excitement and discuss their discoveries, I nudged their investment up to the next quantum level. As Hawkins says,

> *This is again something very different from the stereotype of the permissive classroom because what's involved all along is a teacher who is making* educational capital *out of the interests and choices of children and out of the accidents that happen along the way, as well as out of his own cleverly designed scheme for getting something new into focus.* (1973; emphasis author's)

THE COLLECTIVE UNCONSCIOUS

When I was seven years old, my favorite activity was stream damming. Children around the world share this fascination of making small worlds, shaping the forces of nature in miniature or, as Edith Cobb says, "making a world to find a place to discover a self" (1959). The making of small worlds is one of the deep themes of childhood, the kind of thing that good teachers know you can make "educational capital" out of on a regular basis. The strange fascination with dinosaurs in first grade and horses for fourth-grade girls are other examples of oddly persistent and widespread deep themes. Though it's valuable to speculate about the psychological rationale for these themes at

different ages, it's more important just to recognize that they exist and try to use them in planning the curriculum.

Certainly these features overlap, and it is likely they contradict each other, but when enough of them are present, the possibility of authentic curriculum's making an appearance is heightened.

TAXONOMIC DIFFERENTIATION

Let me place authentic curriculum within the context of other approaches to curriculum. First of all, I don't want my advocacy of authentic curriculum to be confused with support for a laissez-faire, free-school approach that lets the children do what they want to do. Though a certain openness and responsiveness to children is necessary to prepare the conditions, there's a prominent role played by the teacher in shaping what happens. It's like the martial arts principle of taking your opponent's force and using it to accomplish your ends.

Maya Apelman, in her article "On Reading John Dewey Today," summarizes nicely my own general convictions about the role of the teacher vis-à-vis the curriculum.

> *Dewey said that advocates of what had come to be known as the "child-centered curriculum" tended to abdicate their responsibility as adults whose wider knowledge and experience should facilitate the child's entry into the world of people and things, of the present and the past. Today the same tendency exists among some teachers. Many of the young "anti-establishment" people who go into elementary school teaching refuse to assume the responsibility and authority which must be a part of any mature person's functioning. "There is no point in...being more mature," Dewey wrote, "if instead of using his greater insight to help organize the conditions of the experience of the immature, he throws away his insight." (1975)*

On the other hand, teachers held captive by mandated curricular programs enforced by rigid testing schedules certainly won't be inclined to abandon district guidelines to do clay modeling when the children are supposed to have learned thirty sight words by Christmas. Joel Greenberg captures this ethos nicely in critiquing school districts' love affair with packaged curriculum and planning initiatives.

> *The package reduces the teacher to the role of disseminator of specialized, research materials and to the role of transmitter of programmed, planned ways of using these materials. While they may originally have been born of the observed needs of children, they are disseminated wholesale.... Even what is called "individualized instruction" is commonly doled out this way, the concept having been diluted to "type of individual" or, more simply, to rate of instruction with identical material. (1977)*

What we are seeking, in terms of informed curricular practice, is an artistic balance between curriculum structure and objectives and an openness in achieving these objectives. To accomplish this balance, objectives need to be stated in such a way that they don't imply an inflexible time structure—the need to cover all the material—so that when fortuitous serendipity strikes, it can be attended to and not ignored. Hawkins clarifies that Dewey was a strong advocate of this perspective.

> *Dewey, for example, is very strong in asserting that the Experimental School, which he ran for a time, had a definite curriculum and there was no freedom to depart from this curriculum. This was imposed: it was a pattern that could be argued about, it wasn't sacrosanct, but at any given time there was a curriculum and everybody understood what it was. Within this, the teachers were enormously free to pursue these general subject-matter situations in any way they wanted to and it was quite clear also, to many of them at least, that an important group involved in making those decisions was the children themselves.*
>
> *If you read some of the accounts of what some teachers and some children in that school did, you can see that they were having a great good time making their way through some aspect of the curriculum but diverging all over the place. They were diverging into other areas that were also on the curriculum and nobody regarded it as a waste of time, therefore, if in the process of studying some primitive society they got heavily involved in the craft of pottery, because that was also part of the curriculum. (1973)*

Thus, authentic curriculum is most likely to crop up in a classroom where the teacher manages that delicate balance between what Whitehead called "the rhythmic claims of freedom and discipline" (1967). Much good practice that exists in today's schools illustrates this artistry, but let me try to define how authentic curriculum is either a subspecies of other popular progressive approaches to curriculum, or perhaps an altogether different emergent species.

DEVELOPMENTALLY APPROPRIATE CURRICULUM

Much of the valuable curriculum innovation since the seventies has come about through an application of Piaget's work and a recognition of the organic learning processes in childhood. Originated in England as the language-experience approach to reading, Whole Language and The Writing Process have revolutionized and humanized reading and writing instruction in many American schools. The Nuffield Mathematics project, which came out of British primary education, was translated and made more accessible in the Math Their Way and Math: A Way of Thinking books and approaches. The British MacDonald 5/13 Science curriculum series is still one of just a few science curriculum projects to tie program objectives to Piagetian stages rather than to specify content objectives by grade level as is done in the vast majority of American science curricula.

While I am a devout supporter of all these curriculum initiatives, it seems important to note that the major emphasis has been on children's cognitive development in each of these innovations. With subtle accuracy, each of these curriculum approaches has articulated stages of cognitive development and keyed instructional approaches to the unfolding process of logical thinking. What's missing, however, is a sense of affective development, a recognition of the developmental themes that dominate in children's inner lives. Erik Erikson, Robert Kegan, Howard Gardner, Joseph Chilton Pearce, and Rudolf Steiner are a few of the developmental theorists who have charted the inner lives of children, but very little of this understanding has made an impact on curriculum planning.

Many teachers intuitively migrate toward topics of native interest to children, but few can articulate the deep, developmental rationale for why children are intrigued. There is little sense of the connection, for instance, between children's natural interest in geographic exploration, of exploring the boundaries of their immediate world around ages nine and ten, and the appropriateness of studying the Explorers in fifth grade. The Waldorf Schools curriculum, based on the writings of Rudolf Steiner, is one of the few models of curricular topics chosen because of the fittedness with the development of the inner life of the child.

Authentic curriculum is distinct from developmentally appropriate curriculum in tapping into the affective and emotional lives of children. I certainly am not advocating for one to the exclusion of the other; rather I am suggesting that there is a potential basis for curriculum planning other than just cognitive stages of development. Sylvia Ashton-Warner's (1963) "key word" method is a good example of an instructional approach based on emotional rather than cognitive realities. Her use of individualized sight words for beginning reading, different for each child, chosen on the basis of which words were most laden with strong feeling for the individual, is a good example of authentic curriculum.

INTEGRATED OR THEMATIC CURRICULUM

Whitehead's mandate that we "eradicate the fatal disconnection of subjects which kills the vitality of our modern curriculum" (1967) has been taken to heart by those educators that advocate integrating the language, math, science, and social studies curriculum areas through themes and projects. Dorothy Paull, describing the myriad examples of environmental education work done in her British classroom, says,

> *By the middle of the autumn term in 1969, most of the children were working on environmental materials they had brought into the room. They often described their work in prose or poetry, thus bringing together many of the traditional disciplines such as reading, history, geography and, of course, writing. Many of the things that were going on in the classroom tended to erode boundaries between disciplines. Nothing eroded them faster than the stream table. (Paull and Paull 1972)*

Integrated curriculum strives to contextualize learning, to encourage children to see the connections between home life and school learning, to provide situations in which mathematics needs to be done to solve a real problem. But in the name of integrated curriculum, the same exclusion of the children can happen. Teachers dutifully plan integrated themes that require writing and math problems and appropriate science experiments all related to preparing food for the harvest supper, but in their haste to do everything, serendipity is prohibited.

In their book, *Yesterday I Found*, Dorothy and John Paull describe two curriculum projects for nine- to eleven-year-olds: one on bones, the other on mold. Dorothy explains that the bones project began when, without any forethought, she brought some X-ray plates into the classroom and they were discovered by some students. What emerged was a project, at first anchored by one child's interest, that involved a variety of drawing, reading, skeleton reconstruction, owl pellet dissection, and art projects that persisted on and off for many months.

In contrast, Dorothy and John did extensive preparation in the form of background reading, materials preparation, and trial experiments before introducing the mold project (as in molds and fungi) into the classroom. Soon after the project began, the children's interest waned and the whole thing was abandoned. John Paull theorizes why the project didn't work:

> *It seems that I made the error of taking the fun of full investigation out of the hands of the children and the teacher. I designed the containers; I read all the exciting books. For me this was a rich learning experience that developed when the Elementary Science Study booklet aroused my curiosity. I made the mistake of assuming that the children and teacher would react as I did. The episode showed me clearly the difficulties of "packaging" an idea away from the context of the classroom it will be worked out in.* (Paull and Paull 1972)

As well intended as some curriculum planning is, integrated or not, the proof is in the pudding of individual interests and the group chemistry of each class. One year the unit on bones might captivate a group of fourth-grade children for six weeks; the next year with a different group of fourth graders, it might be ho-hum and things will be done by the end of the second week.

The clue to authentic curriculum is recognizing the innumerable variables at work in determining whether something will catch fire or not. To allocate and allot specific time blocks for all the units of study during the course of an academic year ahead of time is asking for trouble. There must be space for the spontaneous fruiting of some unplanned-for project and for the abandonment of a well-planned unit that has worked in the past. This is not, however, an argument for not planning. Louis Pasteur said, "Spontaneity favors the prepared mind." The better prepared you are, the more likely it is that the bird will show up in the window at just the right moment.

BACK TO THE CLASSROOM

Let us move back into the landscape to explore some tangible examples of authentic curriculum at different grade levels and emerging from different sources.

The Loch Ness Monster Project

The Loch Ness Monster project emerged out of the cultivated interest and fascination of one child. Kelly, a third grader in Jane Miller's vertically grouped first-through-third-grade classroom at The Harrisville School, was constantly intrigued with the Loch Ness monster. She brought in newspaper articles, she got books out of the library, and she talked about it at morning meeting. Miller supported the interest, encouraging Kelly to pull together whatever information she could find into a report. Working at the school at the time was an artist-in-residence doing a variety of projects with children. Miller hitched him up with Kelly and the result was a simple animated film describing the various hypotheses about the size and origins of the Loch Ness monster.

Kelly then thought that maybe she'd like to make a model of the serpent, not just a model out of Plasticine, but a life-size model. Since the consensus of all the scientific estimates was that the monster was fifty feet long, this presented a bit of a problem. But Miller forged ahead. The school maintenance workers had just finished painting the school and had a few spare days. Jane enlisted their help in making a wooden frame that they covered with chicken wire, but they decided to compromise on size and make it a half-scale model—only twenty-five feet long. Now everyone got involved. All the children in the class helped to cover it with a skin of polyethylene plastic, make the eyes, nose, and mouth, paint scales on the sides, and generally make it into a fearsome-looking monster.

Speculating on what should happen next, Jane and the artist-in-residence decided that they should surreptitiously slip it into the local mill pond, under cover of darkness, and send press releases to the local papers indicating that because Nessie was so tired of being harried by scientists in Loch Ness, she had decided to relocate to Harrisville, New Hampshire. The children helped to work out the details of the story.

A local reporter and photographer showed up the next day to take pictures, interview Kelly, and write the story. The Associated Press wire service picked up the story and the whole curriculum project was described on front pages around the country. Within a few days, copies of the article from the *Jacksonville Herald*, the *Phoenix Sun Times*, the *Tacoma Daily News*, and a myriad of other places arrived at the school, sent unsolicited by tickled readers. They all said approximately the same thing. "It's great to read this kind of good news in the paper. Keep up the good work. We thought you'd like to know your story made it all the way here."

Miller capitalized on the opportunity. She posted a large map of the United States in the classroom, identified the location of all the places where the class received letters

from, and they were off on a United States geography unit. Some of the children sent thank-you notes, others decided to research other scientific mysteries. Kelly was a little overwhelmed by all the attention.

This no doubt is one of those once-in-a-blue-moon examples. As with the little acorn that grows into the stately oak, it's important to recognize that for every acorn that makes it, another 999 never germinate and rot, are eaten by squirrels, or grow into saplings only to be shaded out by other trees. But the experience of just one of these kinds of curriculum projects during a school year can have an indelible effect on the attitudes toward learning of a whole class. Note how significantly the teacher's initiative and willingness to support the individual's fascination provided the impetus for each significant jump in scale and commitment along the way. Also note that the presence of the artist-in-residence and the availability and willingness of the maintenance staff at just the right moments made this possible. Finally, recognize the collective unconscious fascination with monsters and mysteries, the creatures in the deeps, the shadow or dark side. Many children pursue understanding creatures like Nessie as a way of dealing with or taking hold of their unnameable fears, their fear of the dark, the fear of the dark side of themselves. The curriculum can provide vehicles for children to give shape to their fears and gain cognitive skills in the process.

BECOMING BIRDS

For two years in the mid-1970s I worked with Follow Thru teachers in the Brattleboro, Vermont, public schools during their School Outdoors week. First-through-third graders came to the summer camp setting at Camp Waubenong to participate in environmental education activities. As a staff, we were committed to not lapsing into conventionalized naming and preaching activities, so we brainstormed how to overcome these barriers.

I have always been resistant to using bird curricula with children. Part of this stems from my own childhood sense that watching and naming birds was dumb. Somehow, it never appealed to me until I was in my early twenties. I dislike ardent bird-watchers and environmentalists who try to foist their newfound enthusiasms on unsuspecting six- and seven-year-olds. On the other hand, birds are fascinating and beautiful creatures, and some children are entranced by them. We initiated our curriculum planning by agreeing that we were not going to start our work with birds with the children by trying to get them to identify birds by seeing glimpses of them and then looking them up in books. Rather, we speculated, what is it about birds that appeals to children? It was immediately apparent that the sources of intrigue were (1) they fly and (2) they make nests. Using the developmental principle that children like to become things rather than objectify them in early childhood, we came up with our plan.

We gathered a bunch of refrigerator boxes, cut them into sheets, and had the children lie down on top of them with their arms outstretched. We traced around the children, but instead of following the bottom part of the arm and the upper torso, we drew a straight line from their wrists to their waists then down on both sides to about the knees. The children then stood up, cut out the shape and voilà! an individualized set of wings. We strapped them on to each child, made it clear that they were not to try these out by jumping off roofs, and they were off. A leader and a flock of six to eight birds leaped into action, flying through the forest, exploring life as birds. We made it to the meadow where hay had been cut recently and said, if we're birds, we need nests. And so we made child-sized nests.

The next day we said, "We've been thinking. You guys make great birds, but we noticed that you're all brown and the birds we see around here, well, some of them are brown, but some of them have lots of colors. What are some of the color patterns on birds?" Children described some birds they had seen, we didn't emphasize names, and then we pulled out the paints so they could paint their wings. More bird games followed. About the next day, children started to notice the birds around the camp. "Hey, that's the same bird as me, that's the color pattern on my wings." Then the bird books came out. Soon we had children poring over bird books, trying to identify what kinds of birds they were and learn what they ate. Because we had started at their level of developmental fascination, had engaged their empathy through participating in bird consciousness, they were now ready to objectify and enter the more cognitive realm.

In my course Cognitive Development and Learning Theory at Antioch New England, I encourage graduate students to do research with children. My objective is to try to help prospective teachers get inside the child's world to see how they think and feel and to understand their distinctive developmental ways of organizing the world. One recent project emerged out of a student's childhood memory of thinking she could fly and wanting to try it out when she was a child. She wondered: Do all children go through a stage when they think they can fly? Is there a specific age when children are intrigued with this idea? Though she interviewed only twenty-five children, her findings were intriguing.

Children start to wonder about flying around age four. By age five, they start to wish they could fly, and they start to jump off hummocks and branches to see if anything happens. Many are convinced that if they flap their arms furiously, they stay in

the air just a bit longer than if they don't flap. By six or seven, children want to try it out more seriously. This is when children make wings, climb up on the roof, cast fate to the wind, and sometimes break a leg. By seven or eight, they realize they probably can't fly (except in their dreams), and the interest appears to fade, except for those who go on to be hang-gliders and pilots. The lesson here is that the birds curriculum that we generated tapped into this fairly age-specific fascination with flying. By starting with our perception of children's affective or thematic concerns, we found an avenue of access that brought them into the subject matter. This kind of planning can increase the likelihood of authentic curriculum.

SMUGGLING GOLD

Literature-based reading programs often engage students in personal reflection, discussion, and integrated reading and writing, but teachers rarely take the next steps to extend the themes of a book through dramatic simulation. The following account is drawn from an unpublished paper by Dan Maravell, who completed his graduate internship in teaching in Paula Denton's fifth-grade classroom at The Greenfield Center School in Greenfield, Massachusetts. It illustrates the potential value of addressing the deep themes of secrecy, intrigue, and adventure that emerge strongly in ten-, eleven-, and twelve-year-old children.

In looking for books to help students make sense of their potential role in the Persian Gulf War in 1991, Denton and Maravell chose two books about the Nazi invasion of Europe during World War II. Maravell's group chose to read *Snow Treasure* (McSwigan 1984), a true story about how the Norwegians smuggled their national treasury of gold bullion out of the country and into the United States for safekeeping. Moved from the capital, the gold was hidden in a snow cave near the coast in preparation for it to be moved through the town, down a steep road to a fishing boat hidden at the end of a fjord. The stickiest part of the plan proved to be getting the gold out of the woods down to the edge of the fjord because the Germans occupied the base of the fjord and guarded the length of the road. The solution was to have schoolchildren smuggle the gold on their sleds, making runs right through the ranks of the Nazi guards. Over the course of six weeks, thirty-eight children managed to complete this incredibly risky task.

In consulting with Maravell about how to take this study into children's lives, I suggested we consider the ten-year-olds' fascination with intrigue and personal challenge. How could we translate the challenge into the classroom? Could he somehow set up an activity that would engage the students in the emotional tension and personal riskiness of the story? Following my lead, Dan got his reading group together and formed a secret Defense Club, just as the children in the story had done.

>*My six students and I met out on the landing in the middle of the attic stairs for our next reading period and talked about what we could smuggle, and how it could work. We decided to do bricks and that we had to hide them in the classroom without anyone else knowing, not even Paula, the teacher.*
>
>*One student said that we needed to make a pact to secrecy, to never tell, even if caught and tortured, and we were about to swear to it, hands joined in the center, when another student ran into the room and came back with a wooden sword. We all had to "swear on the old Norse sword," grasping it all together exactly as the children had done in the book.* (Maravell 1991)

Maravell brought the bricks, all wrapped in silver foil, to school in his truck. From there, it was completely up to the students to move the "gold." Maravell appointed one student to be in charge of the Defense Club, just as Uncle Victor, the fisherman, had done in the story. For their first leg, the students decided to move the gold from the truck into the downstairs kitchen.

>*We were checking out various cabinets and around the fridge when a Nazi spy, one of the office staff, came into our midst. She wanted to hang out, say hello, be friendly. The kids were squirming. A couple of foil wrapped bricks had been set down in plain view on the counter. "What have you got there?" she queried. "Oh, we're planning a party and we made some zucchini bread. It turned out pretty good." Four of the students were in the corner, bricks still up their jackets, and they had to move nonchalantly out of the way so the staff person could get into the fridge. Finally she departed.*

From here the children worked in pairs or alone to get the bricks into a seldom-used fabric drawer in the back of the classroom. Numerous problems had to be solved. When the smugglers stayed inside at recess, they were frustrated to find other students who also wanted to stay inside. Some students moved the bricks from the kitchen to way stations closer to the classroom to take advantage of windows of opportunity when the classroom was empty for a few moments. When one student wanted to hide a brick in the chair,

instead of in the fabric drawer, Dan refused to settle the conflict, and made the students resolve it themselves. At the end of the study of the book, which also included a short play and the creation of a newspaper, the students unveiled their accomplishment, much to the amazement of their colleagues and the classroom teacher. Although there had been many close calls, they had pulled it off without a hitch.

The smuggling activity served as the bridge between the Norwegian children and the students in Maravell's classroom. Bonded together by a shared adventure, the students could empathize with the anxiety, fear, ambivalence, and pride that the Norwegian children experienced. The emotional connectedness carried the students into full involvement with the historical facts and problematic issues of war. And it helped the students understand how children in Kuwait and Iraq must have been feeling at that same moment as war raged around them. By finding the connection between the book and fifth graders' personal fascinations, Maravell opened up an avenue into living history and literature. It is this search for the particularities of connectedness between teacher, student, and curriculum that makes for genuine authentic curriculum.

AND SO FORTH

It has been hard to choose the most illustrative examples of authentic curriculum. There is the sixth-grade teacher in Shutesbury, Massachusetts, who starts the school year by taking his students caving. This initiates a semester-long study of underground geography whereby the students study spelunking, draw three-dimensional cave maps, collect rocks, and learn geology. By Christmastime, there's a jewelry-making station set up in the classroom. Students tumble rough semiprecious stones until they're polished, then mount them to make earrings, necklaces, and bracelets that are sold in the Christmas fair. In simulation of age-old rites of passage, the teacher has taken his students through an initiation by taking them down into the earth to find the rough forms of their new selves. These rough selves are polished symbolically into gems, transformed into something of value. The curriculum integrates academic and archetypical themes in an artful fashion.

Or the third-grade teacher in Keene, New Hampshire, who not only read *Paddle-to-the-Sea* (Holling 1941) to her class, but also had each child make a boat just like the boat made by the young boy in the story, with instructions to the finder carved indelibly into each boat. The third graders then walked to the Old Stone Arch bridge over the

Ashuelot River and ceremoniously launched the boats into the oceanbound current. The craftsmanship of each boat was testimony to the fact the boatbuilding connected each child to the story and to the geography that the boat was about to explore. The boat was an embodiment of the developmental fascination, ascendant at eight and nine years of age, with pushing back the boundaries of the known world. These children wanted to know what was beyond their neighborhood, how streams and rivers connected, where the path led—and this curriculum was one small way of addressing those questions. Authentic curriculum assembles the world as it unfolds the self.

COMPLEX SYSTEMS THEORY IN THE CLASSROOM

Some of the current initiatives in the national curriculum arena actually preserve the possibility of authentic curriculum's flourishing in classrooms. The National Council of Teachers of Mathematics has produced a set of standards and curriculum guidelines that sets out the content, skills, and pedagogy it advocates for mathematics instruction in schools. These guidelines, however, "do not contain the content specificity that is common in the national curricula of other countries... and they leave states, districts, schools and teachers enormous room for unique local interpretations" (Smith, O'Day, and Cohen 1990). Knowing that they have a specific destination, teachers are empowered to take curriculum into their own hands and get to the destination by whichever route they choose. Thus, it is possible to take side trips, and respond to the serendipitous bird in the window when it shows up.

But most national curriculum initiatives are not so broad-minded. They tend toward content and method specificity and will enforce their rigid prescriptions with national testing schemes. The mind-set is mechanistic, simplistic, and based on an information-processing paradigm. If we can control input, and demand adherence to standards, then we can guarantee improved output. But classrooms are not like factories and children are not like workers, and the predictive science models of Newtonian physics may no longer be the appropriate metaphoric source for thinking about education.

I have been searching the literature of complex systems theory for new metaphors, new ways of thinking about curriculum dynamics in the classroom. Rather than assuming that classrooms behave like clockwork, let us consider that they work like weather systems, one of the systems that complex systems scientists have been work-ing to understand. Weather systems have classically eluded long-range predictability because they are multivariable systems with a "sensitive dependence on initial condi-tions" (Gleick 1987). With so many interacting variables, slight changes at some dis-tant point can make a major impact in how weather systems will evolve. That is why an ironclad forecast for beautiful weekend weather on Thursday can turn into intermittent showers by Saturday morning.

Classrooms have the same kinds of dynamics. When you factor in twenty dif-ferent personalities, unexpected fights in the hallway, canceled band practices, the unexpected birth of baby gerbils, and eight students absent because of the flu, it's hard to guarantee that your weekly curriculum plans written on Sunday evening will bear much resemblance to the classroom state of affairs on Thursday. It is feasible to stay on track, but sometimes only at the expense of numerous missed possibilities. Certainly teachers need a clear vision of what's appropriate and useful and make choices about the potential productivity of any tangent. But everyone acknowledges that curriculum becomes intriguing, alive, and compelling when something out of the blue captures the imagination of a group of children. Complex systems theory sug-gests that we should recognize the inherent unpredictability of the behavior of such a complex system as a school classroom.

AUTHENTIC SCHOOLS

In a talk entitled "What Should Schools Teach?" Vito Perrone (1988) explores this question of mandating uniformity of content in schools. Professing serious concerns about specifying which facts children should know at the end of which grade, Perrone describes a school in Revere, Massachusetts, where the principal of an all-white school discovered that one hundred Cambodian children would be moving to the town during the next school year. When the children arrived in school, they were met with a warm welcome and outstretched hands of friendship.

The principal and teachers made a decision that it was critical for everyone in the school—children, teachers, custodians, secretaries, lunch workers—to know who these Cambodian children were, where they came from, and why they were coming to Revere. Getting ready for the Cambodian children became the curriculum for the next four months—the reading, social studies, language arts, science, and arts program. It was real, and, as a result it was vital. Those in the school community learned how to speak to the Cambodian children and also gained considerable knowledge about their cultural patterns as well as their suffering. As part of their preparation, those in the school learned about prejudice and the harm that prejudice brings to persons who are different. (Perrone 1989)

Responding to the bird in the window, this school diverged from the habitual curricular mind-set and responded to the unique particularities of its own culture and community.

Submitting to the mind-set that children's brains are like computers just waiting to be programmed will turn our attention away from the local contexts that give meaning to learning. Curriculum as software means that the same program can be downloaded into children's minds at the same time anywhere in the country. But what's relevant to children's lives in Montpelier, Vermont, in January will in some ways be different from what's significant for the same third graders in Tempe, Arizona. The pending change in moose hunting laws in southwestern New Hampshire during 1995 created the opportunity for a rich and complex study culminating in a town meeting simulation in the South Meadow Middle School that year. No prepackaged curriculum existed that was relevant—it had to emerge out of the particularities of the moment. And the immediacy of the problem gave meaning to the learning.

The mind-set of learning as information-processing neglects the role that "meaningfulness" plays in significant learning. Necessity is the mother of invention; inflexible programming is the mother of boredom. Honoring the specific ecology of the life of an individual student, classroom, or school can be the basis for the outbreak of authentic curriculum. As with all endangered species, we need to learn to identify the habitats that authentic curriculum thrives in and protect them from the bulldozers of homogenization. Think of it as our contribution to biodiversity.

CHAPTER 7
VALLEY QUEST
Strengthening Community Through Educational Treasure Hunts

Prelude

While my daughter was growing up, I made it a personal challenge to create a different, developmentally appropriate treasure hunt for each birthday. At six or seven, the children explored the nearby neighborhood. At eleven and twelve, the hunts became more literature based, more problematic, and required the children to travel farther afield. By sixteen, the hunt became less literal and more spiritual, with a theatrical simulation of significant events in my daughter's life to help her identify her personal meaning.

Valley Quest is like birthday party treasure hunts on steroids (to use a currently relevant metaphor). It covers hundreds of square miles, explores centuries of history, and engages thousands of people. Letterboxing USA and Geocaching are two other manifestations of the same fascination. Valley Quest exists at the intersection of the Maps and Paths and Hunting and Gathering design principles. When you go on a quest you have to decipher charmingly crafted children's maps. Part of the challenge is thinking like a fourth grader to understand the map. Conversely, making a map for a quest challenges a fourth grader to think like an adult, to understand how maps work and how to make them followable. The best quests also take you beyond the obvious and into the idiosyncratic nooks and crannies of New England villages. I talked to one couple on a quest with their two- and four-year-old children, who said, "We love questing because it takes us to little hidden corners of New England that we'd never find on our own."

MAPS &
PATHS

HUNTING &
GATHERING

The hunting and gathering here is obviously metaphoric rather than literal, but the same kind of sensitivity to the natural and cultural landscape is cultivated. Creating cemetery quests, students search through town histories, graveyard records, and old deeds to track down information on the Civil War soldiers who are the subject of their project. In natural communities quests, students learn to identify the pinecone middens left by red squirrels, the slide troughs that prove

an otter's presence, the straight-as-an-arrow line of prints in the snow that indicates a fox passed through. They learn the unseen presences so they can open others' eyes to the hidden inhabitants of their town's conservation land. Be forewarned: Questing is infectious. Put down this book and go find one to go on.

IN SEARCH OF THE HOLY VAIL

A raven-haired young woman and her golden retriever gaze out from Port Townsend, Washington's, North Beach over the Straits of Juan de Fuca. Puffy cumulus clouds, squeezed of moisture here in the rain shadow of the Olympics, catch the first rays of the sun on their underbellies. She ponders the meaning of the lines from the riddle in the Tracking the Dragon guide: "Once upon a time, times were so unlike our time that the Waters carried stone on their backs and elephants wore fur coats. In those days the Waters were a pretty hard bunch, sticking together through thick and thin. Eldest Water, a daughter Water, had itchy feet and wanted to wander. Her feet were itchy and very, very big." She notices, up beneath the bluff, a large glacial erratic nestled in the sand. Drawing near, she realizes she's found her prey—a two-foot-long bronze dragon track attached to the sea-washed stone surface. She takes a rubbing of the track and folds it into her rain-stained journal.

Three thousand miles east, the late morning sky is porcelain blue and the maples are doing a pretty good imitation of Dennis Rodman's hairstyle. The fourth graders from the Lyme, New Hampshire, Elementary School are bounding like puppies up the trail to Pinnacle Hill. At the top, they congregate around a sentinel chimney, the only remains of a lonely hilltop cabin, and gaze out upon Smarts Mountain, the Dartmouth Skiway, and the Vermont peaks on the far side of the Connecticut River Valley. They read the last clue:

❖　❖　❖

Facing the chimney's right front edge,

Walk fifty-eight steps to the west,

But take care not to fall off the ledge.

The hiding place is... Have you guessed?

❖　❖　❖

Then, gazing at their compasses, they pace away through meadow grass and sumac saplings. A voice rings out, "I found it! I found it!" and parents, teachers, and kids all stampede to the hollow birch tree, the hiding place of this Valley Quest box.

Vault the intervening ocean, east another three thousand miles. A salt-and-pepper-bearded elderly gentleman wearing wellies, a rain slicker, and a hand-knit woolen cap carefully searches through the rocky clitter on the slopes beneath the promontory of Fox Tor. With a puzzled look on his face, he examines a dog-eared manuscript that cryptically reads: "684451 Tree on hill 320 degrees. Gap between rocks on highest visible point 156 degrees. Box under gorse-covered rock." He examines his Dartmoor map, takes two compass bearings, and grimaces as the mid-afternoon drizzle resumes. He moves upslope, picking his way around lichened, gray stones. Bending over, his arm disappears into a dark hole and then emerges, clutching a battered, WWII–vintage ammunition box. He stands and stretches his stiff back, a satisfied smile warming his damp face.

The Coevolution of Bioregional Strategies

What's happening here? These seekers are all engaged in complex regional treasure hunts where the prize is solving the puzzle and gaining an appreciation of local heritage rather than gold doubloons. Tracking the Dragon is an environmental game and watershed tour created by Wild Olympic Salmon, a community organization dedicated to healthy watersheds for wild salmon and their chums (pun intended). The originator of the game, Mall Peek, joined up with hydrologists, calligraphers, and a host of poets, cartographers, and visual artists to create a series of hunts throughout eastern Jefferson County on Washington's Olympic Peninsula. Placed in diverse watershed locations, each elegantly cast dragon track highlights different slices of the water cycle and the bioregional flora and fauna that depend on healthy ecosystems.

Valley Quest (VQ) is a project of Vital Communities of the Upper Valley (VCUV), an organization committed to revitalizing the sense of community in the individual towns and region of the Upper Connecticut River Valley of Vermont and New Hampshire. VCUV strengthens communities by (1) conducting townwide problem-solving forums, called Community Profiles; (2) identifying and monitoring indicators of economic, social, and environmental health in the region through Valley Vital Signs; and

(3) through fomenting Valley Quest. "Adventures for the Playful, ages three to ninety-three," proclaims the cover of their Quest Guide.

Valley Quest was created by VCUV director Delia Clark, VQ coordinators Maggie Stier and Linny Levin, and a host of local school principals and teachers. (Questing is now a national endeavor promoted by place-based educator extraordinaire Steve Glazer.) Garnering their inspiration from Dartmoor Letterboxing (If you're thinking, "What's that?" just hold your horses), they created an intertown treasure hunt in which teachers and schoolchildren create maps of special places in their towns to exchange with children in other Upper Valley communities. For many teachers and their students, it's a yearlong integrated curriculum that involves going on lots of quests, researching local history, learning mapping skills, interviewing community elders, writing poetry, and discovering new corners of the terrain in their own backyards. The quests lead to hidden treasure boxes in special corners of the community. Underneath all the fun are the serious objectives of creating a good academic curriculum, strengthening collaboration between school and townsfolk, and building a foundation for children's future engagement in civic life. Delia Clark explains, "Children who have gone on quests are more likely to turn into adults who vote, volunteer on town committees, and work to preserve the unique character of their communities."

The grandmother of regional treasure hunts is something called Dartmoor Letterboxing. Dartmoor, of *The Hounds of the Baskervilles* fame, is a high, boggy, rocky, treeless terrain in Devon, England. Covering hundreds of square miles, these unpopulated hills are mostly designated as national park, except for one section that serves as a military reservation. It's always been a popular destination for *trampers* (we know them as walkers or hikers) and somewhere in the middle of the last century a curious tradition emerged. Letterboxes (mailboxes) were established at two or three of the most inaccessible spots on the moor, such as Cranmere Pool. By leaving your letter there, you could get it postmarked from this exotic location. This tradition persisted for a century or more, until some Devonshire folks decided that it would be fun to expand the idea. People hid old weatherproof ammunition boxes, identified their locations with ordinance survey coordinates (similar to longitude and latitude coordinates) and gave some additional directions. Inside was a handmade stamp, an ink pad, and a guest book to show who'd been there. The locations of all these boxes were collected, put into a clandestine catalogue, and lo and behold, a recreational pastime flourished.

After a few years, there were about a hundred boxes spread about. By the time I was in Devon in 1987, the catalogue contained about a thousand boxes. Due to concerns about ecological damage to the moor, dissension flared between the National Park authorities and the troops of bootclad letterboxers. So the development of a letterboxing code of behavior (i.e., fasten all gates; safeguard water supplies; avoid damaging fences, hedges, and walls) educated boxers to the ethic of Moor Care and Less Wear and a truce was reached. The most recent estimate is three thousand boxes, hidden in, on, and around Dartmoor. Hundreds can be found in pubs and other shops. Some letterboxes travel with their creators, appearing only when the right password is spoken. There are sets of boxes that lead searchers to prehistoric tin mines, another set on bridges, another at good birding sites. To find these, you might have to do a bit of research in the classic *Crossing's Guide to Dartmoor* (Crossing 1965) and soon you find that you've learned a lot of British history without sitting through any dull lectures. And the individual box creators who write the poetry, carve the stamps, and maintain the locations sustain it all. Thanks to our Devonshire brethren for this model of nonhierarchical, low-cost family recreation.

VALLEY QUEST TAKES ROOT

It was this families-having-fun-together aspect that intrigued those of us who met to design the educational component of the Vital Communities program in 1995. We wanted something that would help create the strong democracy that makes communities vital, something like the soccer clubs and choral societies that Robert Putnam says provide the fabric of community cohesion. We were familiar with the statistics Richard Louv pulled together for his book *Childhood's Future*—a decrease in family leisure time between 1973 and 1987 from twenty-six hours to sixteen hours per week, parents spending 40 percent less time with their families than twenty-five years earlier, a 14 percent decrease in family vacations from 1983 to 1990. And we were painfully aware of the gradual shift from free-ranging outdoor play to structured indoor recreation. Capture the Flag and Kick the Can were falling prey to the Mario Brothers and all kinds of Nintendo shoot-em-up games. Similarly, organized soccer and hockey meant there wasn't much free time left to build forts and find new fishing spots. We needed an activity that would encourage the exploratory bonding with the earth experiences that are critical in middle childhood—an activity that would, in the words of VQ coordinator Linny Levin, allow children "to learn about places that are right under their noses."

We also knew that we didn't just want this project to be created *for* children. We wanted them to participate in shaping it, and therefore feel some ownership of it. So we took the letterboxing idea and brought it into the classroom, asking teachers and students to work together in choosing the sites and creating the quests. The result is

now more than fifty quests spread over more than fifty Vermont and New Hampshire towns. (Updated to 2007, more than two hundred with new networks being spawned on Martha's Vineyard, in San Francisco, and in your backyard.) We find that the program works best with upper elementary and middle school classes. Here's how it plays out on the ground.

Teachers who make this a yearlong project start by taking their class on already existing quests. That's what Lynn Bischoof's fourth-grade class was doing on Pinnacle Hill. During these first forays, students get a taste of the integrated curriculum that the project offers. In order to complete the quest, children have to follow maps, decode the rhymed clues, use compasses, and apply math skills. For example, after walking the fifty-eight steps west from the chimney, one of the girls looked back and noted, "Three steps is about four feet. Hmmm. Fifty-eight divided by 4." She paused. "I could lie down a bunch of times in a row because I'm 4 feet." From Lyme, this class could go across the river and try the exciting Palisades Quest in Fairlee, or explore the old abandoned village of Quintown during the Flat Rock Quest in Orford, the town just to the north. Through walking and breathing their own history, these children are becoming repositories of local culture.

Back indoors, fourth-grade teacher John Souter in Woodstock, Vermont, started out by engaging his students in learning about maps as the first step in the integrated problem-solving challenge of creating a quest. They looked at panoramic view maps, tourist maps, and street maps of the village. They drew aerial views of classroom objects, made classroom maps, and built models from architectural plans. On the schoolgrounds they made hide-a-penny treasure maps, created treasure maps for their families, and then practiced making small quests for each other in the classroom. Writing rhymed couplets for the clues was a wonderful way to teach poetry in context, in real use in the real world.

Go over the brook and follow the trail,
past tennis courts to the hip roof at Vail.

Keep on going, curve, curve, curve,
white brick building tremendous swerve.

Cathy Ely's fifth-grade class at Ottaquechee Elementary School jumped into the project by focusing on the entire Upper Valley, looking at maps and local geography, calling the local chamber of commerce and trying to figure out what actually determines the boundaries of this loosely defined region. Each student then interviewed townspeople, picked a potential hiding site for their treasure box, and made a presentation to the whole class, trying to sell their site as the one best suited for a quest. Students had to organize notes from research and interviews and create photos, maps, or model displays of their site.

After the site is chosen, the students create the box. Sometimes Tupperware, other times handcrafted, the box is hidden but not buried. It contains a handmade stamp that expresses the significance of the site, an ink pad, a sign-in logbook, and a bit of history or stories about the place devised from the children's research. At the end of the Shaker Village Ritual Site Quest in Enfield, New Hampshire, the Girl Scouts let you in on the secret nineteenth-century ceremony that transpired in this hilltop grove.

Upon completion or revision of all the quests by April, they are all assembled in the Valley Quest Guide and the season officially opens. Everyone and their grandmothers go questing. Cub Scout groups and family reunion parties go questing. Historical societies and conservation commissions bring their memberships on quests. Summer quest fests encourage vacationing honeymooners to join in the fun. During the summer of 1998, Cheryl Taggart, Mark Mullins, and their two children and German shepherd became the first family to complete all thirty-nine of the existing quests in about two months. Woodstock teacher John Souter claims, "It's a real motivating sort of thing. It's pulled together the whole Upper Valley. We've had schools from all over come to do our quests."

After the logbooks have been in place for a season, they provide testimony to the creators' success. One quester commented, "It is a holistic experience—using mind, experiencing the weather...[Children] have to observe and think. It involves the head, heart and hands. I really appreciate that. It is something for children to do that is magical, not materialistic. The experience is what you take away, not a thing."

NEW HORIZONS

It's clear that Valley Quest strikes a far-ranging nerve. After hearing Vital Communities director Delia Clark describe Valley Quest, a Vermont writer decided to write an article about Dartmoor Letterboxing and its New England cousin. The resulting April 1998 *Smithsonian* article spawned a Letterboxing USA movement that has

spread like wildfire (or like a computer virus) across the country. At their website (www. letterboxingusa.org), you can find maps and clues to hunts in almost every county in every state.

Dick Norton, a retired physician and Appalachian Mountain Club member, came upon the Upper Valley Quests and decided to create some in his own hometown. South Shore Quests now invite explorers to hidden corners on Wompatuck State Park in Hingham, Massachusetts, and other conservation land in the area.

The National Park Service's River and Trails Program created a link between Valley Quest and the Southern Rhode Island Green Trail initiative. To educate the public about the wonders of South County, a coalition including the Charlestown Chamber of Commerce, the National Wildlife Refuges of Rhode Island, the South Kingston Land Trust, and the Cross Mills Public Library are working to create quests along the Green Trail. The objective, according to David Monk of the Salt Ponds Coalition, is to diversify recreational opportunities away from the beach. His NPS (National Park Service) grant application, written in true-to-form doggerel poetry, explains:

❖   ❖   ❖

Some Rhode Island groups near the ocean

For beaches and ponds have devotion

But tourists galore

Come visit our shore

Which causes environmental commotion

We want to protect our beach bounty

In the area known as South County

By mapping Green Trail

O'er hill and down dale

We lead guests to scads of green country.

❖   ❖   ❖

The magic of Valley Quest and all these other regional treasure hunts exerts an infectious appeal. We're all compelled to follow the faint tracks to the hidden grail of meaningful engagement with land and community. We feel emboldened when we throw off the shackles of electronic media. As one Tracking the Dragon sleuth said,

What I have enjoyed most about Tracking the Dragon is the opportunity to become, not childish, but childlike, once again. For a brief period of time, the distinction between adults and children has blurred, and we're all, the eight of us, childlike friends pursuing a yearlong gigantic scavenger hunt. We've been able to rekindle our sense of wonder, spend some good times with our families and friends exploring this wonderland in which we live, and we've all had a tapestry of rich experiences in the process.

Won't you come too?

CHAPTER 8
THE SKY ABOVE, THE INTERNET BELOW

Prelude

This essay doesn't focus on any of the specific design principles, but it does examine some of the interesting research and thinking on how computers shape children's relationship with the natural world. And it takes some of the issues introduced in Chapter 4, "Take Back the Afternoon," and goes deeper.

ADVENTURE

One of the core premises is that childhood computer use diminishes the range of kinesthetic experiences and collapses full-body coordination into finger coordination. This narrowing of bodily experience has an impact on neurophysiological development. In this regard, the essay glancingly addresses the Adventure design principle that emphasizes the need for children to run, jump, skip, climb, and explore. Clearly, there's a correlation between increased electronic recreation and increased childhood obesity. Some of the blame can be placed on fast foods, but more video games, more time on task, less recess, more fear of tick- and mosquito-borne diseases, and more fear in general mean that children move less, have fewer adventures, and get fatter faster.

Have you also noticed that the temperature at which children cannot go out to recess has increased over the past decade? In New Hampshire, the average is now about twenty degrees Fahrenheit. (In Canada, it's zero degrees Fahrenheit.) I think there's an assumption that being outside when it's cold is more likely to make you sick despite research on Scandinavian preschoolers that suggests the opposite. And whatever happened to walking to school? It used to be that if you lived within a mile or a mile and a half of school, you didn't get school bus service. Now it's almost considered a crime to make children walk a quarter of a mile. Incrementally, children lose the opportunities to be in their bodies and have few unexpected adventures—like meeting up with a snapping turtle or hiding out to surprise your sister as she comes past the big maple on the walk home from school.

Respecting the children and nature design principles means allowing children moments of unscheduled outdoor time when unexpected bits of life can unfold.

THE SKY ABOVE, THE INTERNET BELOW

The autumnal blush of the honeyed hillsides mirrors the inner glow that my son, Eli, age eleven, and I feel as we drive home from our afternoon of white water kayaking and canoeing on the West River in southern Vermont. The release level was higher than usual that day, the water pushier. It was definitely the biggest water he had ever paddled, and he handled it like a trooper. We were in separate boats—he in a snappy Dagger Dynamo kayak, me solo in my Blue Hole canoe. After he dumped and his boat got carried downstream and collected by a fellow kayaker, I thought he'd be ready to call it quits. But he was ready to jump back in the saddle. It was completely fulfilling to watch him bouncing over the standing waves, playing follow the leader with another accomplished kayaker through the rock gardens, surfing small pillows of water. He's got the beginning touches of that graceful mutuality of boat and water. I anticipate bringing these images back to my mind when he's sitting in front of the screen zapping some enemy into pixilated oblivion.

As we roll toward Brattleboro we talk about upcoming trips planned at his school. He's jealous that the seventh graders, the next class above his, get to go on a backpacking trip to one of the AMC huts in the White Mountains. And he's surprised that his friend Austin isn't very enthusiastic about going. "Austin says it's going to be too much work, too much just being out in nature. I'd love to go, I think it sounds awesome."

Eli's an outdoorsy kid who's into skiing, biking, and fort-building. We parse out a limited diet of computer gaming, Internet browsing, and television—not more than an hour a day all together. Austin is a great soccer player, smart as the proverbial whip, and is a partner in a little computer start-up company. "Local Youngsters Start Web Development and Consultation Firm" read the headline in the August issue of our community newsletter. Along with a couple of other local boys, they've started Awesome Technologies, a web-page development firm, and one of their first jobs is to design a site for our local town government. One of the selectmen said, "We are delighted with Awesome Tech's proposal and are pleased to support this youthful enterprise. We admire the boys' entrepreneurial skills and look forward to working with them." I admit to twinges of parental angst when the article came out. "Why isn't Eli involved in this? Is he lacking in computer literacy? Will he be left behind while his friends swoop onward in the new postindustrial dotcom economy?"

It's a tough job for a parent to swim against the current of computerization in our children's lives. It's similar to Just Saying No to soccer. Especially travel soccer. In rural New Hampshire, travel soccer means that a good chunk of one or both weekend days are spent on the road for hours, plus a couple of afternoon practices during the week. I mean, I love soccer. I think it's the best kid sport in the world, but I fear the all-consumingness of it. Just like I fear the whirlpool effect of electronic recreation. So I resist the pull of soccer and electronic recreation in favor of preserving the primacy of my children's relationship with nature.

The subtext became clear to me a couple of weeks ago. My daughter needed a bit of information for some school project and we quickly browsed the Internet to find it. "Technology is so awesome!" she commented under her breath. *Awesome.* There was that word again, echoing in the name of the Internet company and in Eli's comment about backpacking in the White Mountains. Then I noticed the counterpoise: wilderness experience as awe-inspiring versus the wedding of mind and machine as the source of awe. There's an eerie transformation going on here. The crash of thunder is giving way to the crinkle of shrink-wrap. Our children are getting their first glimpses of God by going into cyberspace rather than up onto the mountaintop.

I remember a cooking project I did with a bunch of first graders many years ago. To take advantage of all the parents' abundant garden produce, we made fresh tomato soup as a morning project and served it with lunch. "How's the soup, Amanda?" I asked cheerily, proud of our organic curriculum. "Well, it's good," she responded hesitantly, "but I think I like *real* tomato soup better. You know, the kind that comes in a can." Reality in a can, or on a DVD.

A recent set of research studies suggests the implications of this transformation. Interested in exploring the effect of virtual nature experiences on natural nature experiences, environmental psychologists Daniel Levi and Sara Kocher conducted studies with eighty-seven college students at California Polytechnical Institute in San Luis Obispo, California. They report their findings in "Virtual Nature: The Future Effects of Information Technology on Our Relationship to Nature" in *Environment and Behavior.* Here they describe how they presented students with images of classically beautiful scenes of nature and local natural environments, varying the sequences for different groups, and then interviewed the respondents about their attitudes toward the places represented. From two of their studies with linked results, they drew some disturbing conclusions. The study found that "the commercial media's presentation of nature tends

to cause people to devalue their emotional experience of local natural areas" (2000). The following study suggested that "one of the effects of simulated nature experiences is to increase support for the preservation of national parks and forests, but it decreases support for the acquisition and preservation of local natural areas." The Wilderness Society might be happy to hear this, but when your community tries to buy the development rights on that old eighty-acre farm, you might not find a constituency.

The long-term trend, Levi and Kocher suggest, is that

> by using virtual nature to satisfy our psychological desires we become less aware of what we as humans are doing to our environment... For example, experiencing nature only in virtual environments may disrupt our physiology because of the lack of exposure to natural daylight. As we become less aware of the changes in our local natural environments, we may not perceive the health-threatening changes in air or water quality that are occurring in our environment." (2000)

It's the logical extension of one of the hidden curriculum messages that Internet browsing encourages in schools: that which is virtual and far away is significant and important; the nearby and local, the communities of people and plants outside the door, are parochial and boring.

A September 2000 report by the Alliance for Childhood entitled *Fools' Gold: A Critical Look at Computers in Childhood* takes the bull by the horns. In the Executive Summary, the authors contend that

> computers pose serious health hazards to children. The risks include repetitive stress injuries, eyestrain, obesity, social isolation and, for some, long term physical, emotional, or intellectual damage. Our children, the Surgeon General warns, are the most sedentary generation ever. Will they thrive spending even more time staring at screens? (Almon et al. 2000)

This comprehensive and well-documented report assembles findings from hundreds of studies conducted over the past decade, casting critical light on the "politics of technomania." Is it really wise, they question, to reduce recess, field trips, and art and music education to provide more time and resources for technology education?

For instance, software simulations of nature are now serving as substitutes for live field trips to local rivers and parks—it's so much less messy. But these simulations reduce children's actual contact with the real world rather than increasing it. A report from the U.S. National Science Board in 1998 cautioned, "Computing and cyberspace may blur children's ability to separate the living from the inanimate, contribute to escapism and emotional detachment, stunt the development of personal security, and create a hyper-fluid sense of identity" (Almon et al. 2000). Sherry Turkle, an MIT sociologist, illustrated this problem when she recounted her young daughter's comment on seeing a jellyfish for the first time, "But Mommy, it looks so realistic." Anyone want Campbell's tomato soup for lunch?

Consider, for example, how computer use might interfere with the complex matrix of physiological development in childhood. The way children use their hands is changing as a function of increased computer use. Instead of grasping tree limbs and paintbrushes, pulling weeds, delicately handling butterflies, throwing acorns, and holding onto the merry-go-round for dear life, fingers are used more and more for tap-tap-tapping. The wide range of motions for which the hand is programmed is getting constricted to a narrow repertoire of movements. Consequently, the diversity of development of neural pathways is also diminished.

Neurologist Frank Wilson, medical director of the Health Program for Performing Artists at the University of California School of Medicine at San Francisco, has summarized the research on the integration of physical experience and brain development in his book, *The Hand: How Its Uses Shapes the Brain, Language and Human Culture.* Joan Almon and her colleagues summarize his contention that

the evolution of the human brain over millions of years has been inextricably linked to the ways in which humans use tools. Changes in the structure of the human hand and arm, related to the need to grasp, throw, and manipulate objects like stones and sticks, led to changes in the structure of the brain and nervous system and the development of more complex patterns of thinking... This same process of co-evolution takes place in the development of individuals: children who learn to play the violin or piano, for example, develop neural networks that affect their ways of learning throughout life. And Wilson speculates that the individual infant's potential to develop incredibly refined and related hand and language skills may be a combined, "elemental force in the genesis of what we refer to as the mind, activated at the time of birth." (2000)

Grasping with the hand, he suggests, facilitates grasping with the mind. Groveling around in the soil develops your ability to conceptually root out ideas. If our fingers continually just float above the keyboard, our minds will similarly just drift across the surface, never settling down, never developing a sense of place.

But, of course, this is what all the alarmist adults say. What do kids think about how their computer/Internet time shapes their relationship with nature? When I spent a half hour with sixth graders in Putney, Vermont, I was surprised at how much they had to say. These kids live in an idyllic woods-and-farms rural community, but computer and other electronic recreation is a big part of many of their lives. One girl sheepishly admitted, "Before we had a computer, I used to read a lot and go outside more to be in the neighborhood. Now, it's so easy to go exploring on the computer, it's like it's too much work to go outside." Another boy agreed, "I'll be playing a really cool computer game and I'll think, 'Wow, it's beautiful outside, I should really go outside.' But I can't stop myself from playing, it's kind of like I'm addicted." Another student countered, "Well, my sister's like that, but not me. I like being outside all the time. I can only spend about fifteen minutes on the computer, because after that, I get really bored." And, pulling all the threads together, one student summarized, "For me, I learned to love nature before I did computers, and so it doesn't really affect me. But if I started to use computers when I was really young, it might have kept me from getting into nature."

An interesting conversation developed around virtual dirt-bike-racing games like Moto-Cross and Moto-Racer—favorites of some of the boys. Does playing Moto-Racer on the computer encourage you to go out and tear up the woods on a real dirt bike? One boy straightforwardly said that he liked to ride dirt bikes *and* play dirt-bike computer games; there really wasn't much difference. But a friend of my son's said that he didn't think there was any relationship. "There's not really any connection between the virtual game and riding real dirt bikes. The game is so unrealistic. Like in the game when the guy falls off the bike he just goes, 'Oooff,' gets up, dusts himself off, then gets back on the bike. If that really happened, you'd be seriously injured. For me, it's just a game."

When we wound back to the topic of being addicted to the computer, all the students were quick to point out that lots of other things are addictive too. "If you took all these different things—TV, Game Boy, Nintendo and computer games—I think all those things are more addictive than computer games. It's easier to turn the computer off." Didn't John Muir say something about finding out that once you try to separate out one thing, you find that it's hitched to everything else? Can we really isolate out children's Internet and computer experiences from the range of electronic mind candy that seduces them at every turn? Maybe it's like trying to differentiate between vodka, whiskey, and gin—they'll all get you drunk.

But lest we wax nostalgic for the good old days, I offer up a cautionary tale from one of the Putney, Vermont, students. "When my mom was young, she loved watching the *Mary Poppins* movie over and over again. She wanted to *be* Mary Poppins. So one day when her mom wasn't around, she got an umbrella, climbed up on the roof, jumped off, and broke her leg." I guess it's a good thing Mary Poppins wasn't into dirt-biking. On the other hand, growing up in the era of Mary Poppins, I saw maybe ten movies a year and spent a lot of time throwing snowballs at cars, beachcombing, and exploring the local haunted house. Nowadays for children, it's ten movies a week and a tidal wave of email, *Deer Hunter*, *Tomb Raiders*, and *Who Wants to Be a Millionaire*. Perhaps the only viable solution is moderation in all things, and at least as much real reality as virtual reality. Anyway, I've got to wrap up. My son is bugging me to let him use the computer.

CHAPTER 9
ISLAND PLAY
Disney World Is Like a Flea Compared to Whitehead

Prelude

Sometimes it's refreshing for play not to be in the service of learning. In many of these essays I'm guilty of harnessing play to teach social studies or eco-logical concepts or to make writing better. Here I enjoy watching play unfold for its own sheer joy.

The design principles abound here. The Whitehead Game is a complex syn-thesis of the Adventure, Hunting and Gathering, and Maps and Paths prin-ciples. It comes out of a decades-old commitment to honoring these aspects of childhood. In other words, it didn't just appear, it was designed by adult creators attempting to craft a form that acknowledged the deep impulses of boys.

Similarly, Merchants and Pirates owes its existence to cultural history and a unique set of environmental factors. This wide-ranging horseback game depends on a sophisticated Maps and Paths understanding and a spirit of Adventure and is enhanced through its emphasis on Fantasy and Imagination.

Mailboat Skits are pretty much just pure fun and are motivated purely by Fantasy and Imagination. They are a great example of adults and children being silly together.

The deeper essence that holds all these together is the power of complex play to connect children to places. I'm convinced that these games are the medium for a number of transcendent experiences that won't be articulated until these children are looking back on the formative experiences in their lives. And I've personally seen how these immersive games have led to lifelong environmental ethics in adults who fondly remember them.

ADVENTURE
◆

FANTASY & IMAGINATION
◆

MAPS & PATHS
◆

HUNTING & GATHERING
◆

EUREKA!

We're sitting at long tables in the old Coast Guard Station barracks on Whitehead Island in Penobscot Bay. Between mouthfuls of Rice Krispies or Cheerios, little dribbles of milk running down their chins as they chew and talk simultaneously, Brady, Nicco, Frank, and USA (a sandy-haired kid named after his logo'ed T-shirt) are recounting great moments in yesterday's Whitehead Game. "We tried coming in from different directions a million times. From there, there, over there," Frank complains. He uses his hand, his elbow, his chin to gesture out the windows toward the starting points for all those attacks. "The last time, I would have made it, but my pants fell down so I tripped and went down right by the picnic tables."

Brady commandeers an abandoned cereal bowl to represent the circle of rope that surrounds the goal. "I was the decoy. I came in, circled around, everyone ran after me. Nicco just stayed quiet in the ferns and when they all followed me, he ran straight in and scored. Burns was hiding behind that old car chassis, but it all happened so fast that he couldn't get in fast enough to stop Nicco."

"Yeah, remember we were sneaking up on Vince to catch him, but then he sees us and says, 'Don't bother, I can't move.' He was stuck so deep in the bog mud that he couldn't get his leg out. Took both of us to pull him out," says USA, proud of his generosity in helping someone on the *other* team.

A wave of recognition tingles through me and I'm back fifteen years ago, with a different group of similarly aged Afro-Caribbean boys deep in a mahogany, gumbo-limbo, and tamarind forest on the side of Cabesair, a pointy island peak. We're hunting iguana on Carriacou, north of Grenada. "He slam to de groun an he puff up, all mad. Dose prickers on his back stickin up." As Dane describes the iguana, he puffs up his cheeks, rounds his back, and rolls back his pupils so all we can see are the whites of his eyes. "I mash him, but he run away in a flash," Hollie adds.

Separated by thousands of miles and hundreds of thousands of dollars of family income in completely different ecosystems, these boys are rapturously telling stories about their island adventures. There's some ancient vein of human experience being tapped into on both islands: the primacy of the hunt, male bonding. And yet, there's a cultural uniqueness. The Whitehead Game is played nowhere else in the world. The weapons used for iguana hunting in this village on Carriacou are unique, the product of local ingenuity and recycled trash. Like Darwin realizing that each island in the

Galapagos has its own distinctive finch, I see that each island has its own distinctive games. Sitting at the breakfast table with sunlight splashily illuminating Tony the Tiger on the Frosted Flakes box, I realize, "I've stumbled upon a new species!"

ISLAND BIOGEOGRAPHY

Darwin's observations in the Galapagos Islands during his four-year journey on the *Beagle* had a significant impact on his ideas regarding natural selection and speciation. As he traveled among the more than twenty islands, he found that though they were close in proximity, they were quite diverse in terms of rainfall, soil development, and other ecological conditions. Similarly, he found very different animals on each of these islands. In some cases, he found animals of the same family, but of strikingly different species. For example, there were finches on many of the islands, but they were all distinctly different as a function of the nature of the diverse habitats and the food sources. Some nested in cacti, others on the ground. Where the food source was predominantly seeds, finches had fat, seed-breaking beaks. Where the food source was insects, finches had narrow beaks suitable for reaching inside the holes or flowers where the insects resided. There were even vampire finches that pecked at ground-nesting boobies to draw blood to drink as part of their diet.

Back in England, Darwin eventually speculated that individuals of one species of finch had arrived from the South American continent many millennia ago, and as the population developed, they spread from one island to the next. Once on an island, natural selection drove the morphology of the original species in unique directions and unique species emerged accordingly. On islands, for instance, where seeds were the predominant food source, finches with fatter beaks reproduced while finches with narrower, less successful beaks didn't survive to have offspring.

This process of speciation in isolated ecosystems has been documented around the world. On the southern coast of the Hawaiian island of Oahu, five distinct species of agate snails inhabit five adjacent valleys, one per valley. Researchers speculate that originally one species of snails wandered into each of the valleys and then subsequently the steep rocky ridges between the valleys served as effective isolating barriers preventing interaction and breeding. Some of the snails are striped, some all golden yellow, some tall, some squat—one species per valley as a function of the unique ecology of that valley.

Linguists speculate that languages evolve in a similar fashion. A population sharing the same language is separated by a natural or cultural disaster. For instance, a volcanic eruption closes off a valley that connects two villages that share the same language. Cut off from any discourse over many generations, the language attributes in these now two distinct natural and cultural environments evolve in slightly different directions. Different dialects, elements of the lexicon, and rhythmic patterns gradually develop so that eventually two related but distinct languages emerge. We see this in regional dialects in the United States in tiny ways—for example, speakers in the Northeast say "soda," and people in the Midwest say "pop." And these unique shared cultural elements tend to bind populations together. When northern New Englanders hear *wicked* used as an enthusiastic amplifier, as in "We had a wicked awesome blueberry crop this year," they know they're among friends.

My contention is that play and recreation follows the same principles of speciation, clearly on islands, but also in culturally and geographically isolated communities. It's especially true where adults and children play together over longish periods of time. In the normal, workaday world, these conditions usually don't exist. But on vacation, at summer camp, or on summer family islands, adults are freed from work responsibilities and can settle back into play consciousness. And children have the freedom to be children, not tethered to programmed sports and often outside the range of electronic recreation.

I got my first sense of this in the 1970s when visiting a friend on the family island of Naushon, one of the Elizabeth Islands at the seaward end of Buzzard's Bay in Massachusetts. The islands, stretching from Woods Hole to Cuttyhunk, have been privately owned for 160 years. (No trespassing, please!) The eastern end of Naushon is settled with about thirty-five houses and a working farm. The western end, about six miles long and a mile wide, is a complex network of old carriage paths and foot trails winding through old-growth beech and holly, copses of locust and oak, open meadows, and shrubby thickets leading to hidden ponds and secluded crescent beaches. It's a remarkably magical landscape. For decades, it harbored a substantial population of sheep that roamed the island freely most of the year as "woolies" until they were all corralled for shearing.

Over dinner one soft July evening, our hostess, Penny, regaled us with stories of the good old days growing up as a child on the island during the summers. Nowadays, family vacations have shrunk to a couple of weeks squeezed in between soccer, tennis, or computer camp. Thirty or forty years ago, Mom and the kids, with Dad coming on weekends, used to spend all summer on the island. Penny described a game called High Seas, and a variation called Merchants and Pirates, which involved traveling between an eastern and a western stone wall across miles of sheepy wilderness. It's still played each August.

The idea is to convey some precious item on horseback from east to west or west to east. Each team has a home base near the boundary wall. They plan to reconnoiter somewhere in the middle at prearranged hideouts to exchange goods. However, they have to avoid the pirates, a third team who commandeer the center of the island, ever watchful for unsuspecting voyagers. Everyone plays, though the number is capped at around thirty because that's as many horses as are usually available. Moms and uncles, daughters, aunts and nieces, young and old are all involved, with high-stress roles reserved for teenagers.

The whole game happens on horseback and involves stealth, breakneck speeds, navigational wizardry, and a well-memorized mental map of the welter of trails, paths, shortcuts, and uncrossable marshes between here and there. I have never heard of a game anything like it. What could explain its emergence here and nowhere else?

Family history, in part. The Forbes family earned some of its early wealth from the China trade, which emerged after China was open to the Western world, and especially American trade, in 1867. Ships traveled from east to west, or from west to east, and one of the major problems was piracy. This China-trade wealth—and later investments in railroads and communications—funded the purchase of the Elizabeth Islands, and access to the houses was mostly limited to extended family members. The lore and language of the ship captains' families perhaps provided the metaphoric archetype for the structure of the game. But there was more. Committed to the idea of preserving the pastoral lifestyle, the family leadership had agreed to no motorized vehicles on the island other than for farm work. Thus, horseback riding and horse-drawn carriages became the primary modes of transportation, which shaped the nature of the paths and roadways. And a large enough group of families, making for about two hundred people on the island at any one time, provided a critical mass of children and adults willing to participate in a game that required lots of participants over a large sprawl of hinterlands.

The combination of family lore, the braided network of paths providing innumerable route options, and the prevalence of a large group of horseback riders were the unique set of ecological factors that led to the spontaneous generation of a unique species of game. Of course, there was something about the islandness of the situation that supported the evolution as well. The boundaries were preset and concrete. There was little likelihood of strangers wandering in, getting in the way or wondering what you were up to. You could get lost for an hour or more, but never seriously. Play requires specifically designed arenas. Tennis has its court, Monopoly its avenues, bowling its alleys, drama its stage. The island of Naushon was the perfect game board—not too small, not too large—for a re-creation of trade on the high seas.

If Naushon had its own game, I wondered, were there other islands, or islandlike isolated communities, with their own endemic species? Lo and behold...

MAILBOAT SKITS

Since then I've been on a quest, albeit a quiet one. Like the Amazonian botanist searching the treetops for new beetles, bromeliads, and amphibians whose toes never touch solid ground, I've poked around on islands trying to unearth unique games. On that same island of Carriacou, as part of Mardi Gras, there's an unusual form of combative Shakespeare. Decked out in spectacularly wild costumes, island men toss lines of Antony and Cleopatra back and forth at each other until one contestant's memory fails. It's an elimination match, with a new section of the play being used for each round.

My favorite novel of all time, John Fowles's *The Magus,* is set on a Greek isle. The main character is roped into a theatrical game created purely for his own ethical edification. He can't tell what's real, what's staged, and he can't pull himself away from playing. The story is unique—based on his current relationship dilemmas and shaped by the role he improvises. The ending isn't predetermined; the path emerges as the story unfolds.

Amid the bleak tors and marshes of Dartmoor in Devon, England, a figurative island of wilderness in southwestern England, I discovered Letterboxing (see also Chapter 7). With its roots in long-distance tramping and isolated British postal boxes, a hide-and-seek game of mammoth proportions has spread itself out across hundreds of square miles of old tin mines, gnarled copses of woods, windswept grasslands. Hundreds of families, scout troops, and pensioners spend each weekend unraveling literary and geographical puzzles in search of rubber-stamp images.

"We Brits can get quite serious about daft things," commented one longtime player.

Which brought me about ten years ago to Three Mile Island, an Appalachian Mountain Club camp on New Hampshire's Lake Winnipesaukee. We'd been planning on going to a little island off the coast of Nova Scotia when a medical problem intervened. Casting about for an alternative, my friend Jack, former head of the New Hampshire Lakes Association, suggested Three Mile, named not for its length but because it was three miles from Center Harbor. (There's also One Mile, Five Mile, and Six Mile Islands—there are 365 islands in the lake so it's hard to come up with an endless supply of interesting names.)

I'd always avoided Lake Winnipesaukee. Too many cigarette boats and all those chockablock houses crowding the shore. And though it turns out to be noisy on weekends, during the week it's really quite placid. Three Mile is an extended-family kind of place, where families and their kids have been coming for years, and kids grow up and bring their families. Most people come for a week. All ninety guests eat together at the main lodge and then there are about forty-five tiny cabins scattered around the edge of the island. Each two-person sleeping cabin is a world unto itself. There's a porch, a tiny private dock, a soft forest of pines and hemlocks, only kerosene lighting. Reading on my porch in the afternoon breeze, I really feel away. On the other hand, there's also the main dock. Complete with recreation hall, boathouse, canoe and kayak racks, waterslide, diving board, and float, this is where the action is during most of the sunlit hours. And this is the seedbed for local creativity.

Local traditions abound. Art in the outhouse, the mile-long swim circuit of the island, water carnivals (diving for coins, canoe tug-of-wars, mixed kid and adult freestyle relays—King Neptune presiding).

But the pièce de résistance, the endemic species of island play that makes Three Mile unique, is the Mailboat Skit.

See it through the eyes of a visitor on a leisurely cruise around the lake as the U.S. Postal Service mailboat delivers letters and care packages to summer camps and island outposts. You sit on the upper deck and listen to the stock tourist patter of the captain. The boat pulls into landings on tidy islands with lake homes and cottages to die for. Docks connected by complex walkways thread out into the lake. You drool over boathouses with more square footage and higher assessments than your whole house. It all looks so cozy, upscale, and woodsy, yet tasteful. After a number of stops, the captain announces you're pulling into the AMC's Three Mile Island Camp. Over the thrum of the engine, there seems to be a louder, harsher rhythm. A metallic, tribal throb assaults your ears as the boat pulls up to the dock. A throng of natives, clothed in leopard skin, clown suits, and ragtag yard sale cast offs, dances in a circle. "Meat to eat! Meat to eat!" they all seem to be chanting. They're gathered around what looks to be a stake, with firewood arranged at the bottom in preparation for conflagration.

From the woods emerge another, smaller horde of natives dragging a struggling victim. She is tall, wears a coconut-shell brassiere and meager skirt, is incongruously

bearded, and is valiantly resisting her fate. Or is it his fate? She or he is tied to the stake and the natives dance convulsively around, urging the flames to leap up. The chanting becomes cacophonous, indecipherable, then suddenly the sacrificial virgin loosens her shackles, fends off her attackers, and dives into the lake. The natives all plunge in behind her and don't resurface. Until they show up, dripping, five minutes later to buy the Frozen Taco ice cream bars that the mailboat sells to amplify its meager sale of stamps.

On a different day, as the boat approaches Three Mile, the captain announces that he's not sure what people do on Three Mile, but they seem to do a lot of hanging around. As the boat pulls in, there's a strange scene on the boathouse. In a frozen tableau, four children are attached to the wall facing the water, as if they're sunbathing on the dock, towels draped over them, but they're hung like pictures. "Just Hanging Around," reads an explanatory banner. The young children look relaxed and comfy, unaware of the onlookers. You gradually realize that they're held in place by beach towels that have been stapled to the wall, like those little envelopes glued to the photo album page that you used to put your stamps in for your stamp collection. The kids don't say anything; it's just a visual vignette.

Some mailboat skits achieve the status of revered tradition and get done over from year to year. Other skits are born fresh out of the minds of lighthearted adults and children with just enough time on their hands to play together. Some skits involve getting a shill onto the boat at Weirs Beach, the origin point for the cruise. All the boat travelers are shocked when one of their own is targeted for some unanticipated indiscretion. But it's all in good humor and over in about five minutes.

It's interesting to trace the evolution of this particular species. Skits have developed as an art form in many of the White Mountain huts of the Appalachian Mountain Club. These high-elevation, isolated, overnight accommodations provide shelter for hikers and serve as islands of comfort amid the cold, windy peaks. As the hut "croo" have to communicate the same boring information to visitors over and over day after day, a tradition emerged of embedding the instructions on how to fold your blankets or how to make hot cocoa correctly inside inventive skits. The costuming, accents, and unanticipated twists and turns of the plot lines before arriving at the nexus of instruction are hilarious. These skits carry over into the culture of Three Mile Island Camp, with hut croo often conveying information in story and song. However, because campers at Three Mile are in residence for a week, rather than just overnight at the huts, they have taken up the skit ethos as well.

The precipitating ecology is the dock scene. The mailboat arrives at Three Mile precisely at noon. The dock is often crowded with swimmers, sailors, kayakers, readers, ping-pongers, and at the end of the morning, everyone is itching for a change of pace, a bit of frivolity. The mailboat's arrival brings a dependable, unsuspecting audience right to the edge of the stage. And thus this combination of cultural tradition and just the right environmental conditions creates the unique species of *Skittus mailboatia*.

Kids who never do theater, adults who would never dress in drag, and affiliations of children and other people's parents who don't really know each other get swept up in the fun. And in the dark of winter, far from the lap of lake water on the summer shores, it's these skits that often get talked about over corn chowder at dinner. They help bond families and bond children to the special world of the summer island. It's my son's favorite week of the year because of the seamless fabric of family, play, and natural world that gets woven together out on the island.

THE WHITEHEAD GAME

Which brings us back to where we started. But first a bit of context. Pine Island Camp is one of Maine's respected, long-standing summer camps for boys, located on an island in the Belgrade Lakes. It was founded in the early 1900s in the heyday of conservation, the emergence of recreational camping, and the founding of the Boy Scouts. One of the early directors of the camp, Dr. Eugene Swan, exhorted the virtues of the simple, vigorous, outdoor life, saying,

> *Young man, get out into the open! The world demands staying qualities. Do not, oh, do not, spend your vacation time in a hotel, or Pullman car… The great cry of "Back to Nature" that is spreading abroad over our land is full of deep significance, and the heeding of Nature's ever-calling voice, and an adaptation of our lives to her laws, is going to become a salvation of the American race.* (Nagler 2002)

In addition, Dr. Swan believed in the inherent value of a childhood lived fully. To encourage the connection between nature and childhood, Dr. Swan conceived of summer camp as an outpost of "Boyville." He said, "Boys live in dreams, and they should always be respected, for out of the dreams of youth have come the world's best gifts." In this spirit, he ran a camp filled with mystery, surprise, complex games, adventure, and the unexpected.

As a result of Dr. Swan's original vision and the pristine seclusion of the camp on an island, a rich gumbo of unique natural and cultural traditions emerged. A whole mythology of kings, sacred animals, and fantastic places flourished. Campers were roused in the middle of the night to participate in sacred rites. The War Game, which covers miles of Maine countryside over a number of days, became the crowning experience of the summer season. The camp, as an outpost of Boyville, respects the imagination, wildness, and exploratory desires of boys and channels these into character-building and nature-bonding experiences. Out of this matrix, the Whitehead Game grew.

Whitehead Island, off Great Spruce Head, south of Rockland, became an outpost of Pine Island Camp in the late 1950s. Pine Island had always had a tradition of expeditions to the mountains and the sea, so Whitehead became a home away from home for campers on the rocky coast. Today, groups of about twelve boys arrive each week with their counselors to explore tide pools, fish, greet each day by plunging into the frigid brine, and play unique games such as Nupple Tucker, Ultimate HAGS, and the Whitehead Game. "Hands down, the Whitehead Game is the boys' favorite," says Anne Stires, the island camp's director.

The parameters: Clearly, Capture the Flag is the rootstock of the Whitehead Game. But there are enough differences to justify its being considered a unique species, especially because it's been adapted to the particularities of the Maine coast. As in Capture the Flag, there are two territories and once you're on the other team's territory, you can be captured. One of the compelling things about the Whitehead Game is that almost the whole of the ninety-acre island (except down by the old lighthouse) is in bounds. As one of the boys said, "It's so large scale. You can go anywhere on the island and it goes on for so long. It's better than Capture the Flag because it's not such a big drag to get caught and then have to go to jail. You just have to go back. So there's a punishment, but not a super big one."

Unlike Capture the Flag, captives from the other team are not put in jail. (Always a sore point when I've played Capture the Flag, and getting free from jail was often the source of endless arguments.) Instead, you've just got to give up your rings (little plastic circles) and then go back to your side. This modification is an example of natural selection trimming off a vestigial limb of the game organism. By eliminating jail, the game becomes more appealing and therefore more likely to survive.

Scoring, as you've figured out, is also different. In Capture the Flag the idea is to go into enemy territory, grab their flag, and then make it back to your territory with the flag. Hurrah! Game over. But in the Whitehead Game, you score points, and the game lasts a looooong time, say, three hours. Each team defends a goal that includes a circle of rope about fifteen feet in diameter and a center pole with hooks. The object is for an attacker to get any part of his body into the circle without being tagged. Then any rings he is carrying get hung on the pole and the points accrue to the attacking team. The precious rings are the little plastic circles left behind when you crack open a half-gallon of Oakhurst ("the natural goodness of Maine") milk, a stalwart of the midcoast dairy industry (and another example of how local flora and fauna make games unique). Different Oakhurst products—quarts and gallons of milk, orange juice, cream—all come with different-colored caps and therefore different-colored rings, providing a panoply of scoring opportunities—green is 1 point, red is 5 points, yellow is 10 points on up to the big enchilada, orange, which is 50 points.

So here I am, embedded, to use modern military journalism parlance, with one of the teams in the Whitehead Game. I'm panting, sweating profusely, crouched down in wet sphagnum, clamped up next to a gnarly spruce, trying not to give away my teammates' location. In true ethnographic spirit, I'm trying to experience the game from the native perspective, and I'm wondering if I have the aerobic stamina to keep up with thirteen-year-old boys, or at least just keep from gasping too loudly.

Lobster boats growl by not far away, buoys gong, and the foghorn bellows in the distance, and underneath all that we listen for the subtle sounds of twig snap and swamp sploosh. But all I can hear is mosquitoes, whining like a really big group of tired four-year-olds, and the delicate sound of my skin being punctured, followed by the slurp of blood. There are gazillions of mosquitoes, no exaggeration, and yet the boys seem to barely notice them. They are immersed in the hunt.

We're up and running again, through alder thickets, log-walking through bogs, slimy lichen skids on rocks, path, no path, then out of the woods onto the cobbly shore, rock-hopping heedlessly. No scenery, all details. We stop to look at a dead baby seal.

Robbie exclaims, "Hey, I've never been here at high tide before. This'd be a good swim spot, just down the shore from the lobster eating place. You should probably hang back through here."

"Are we on their side?" I query.

"Big time."

Screams in the distance merge with wave slap and the calls of whitethroats and goldfinches. The boys decide that Brady will scout ahead while Robbie and Nicco wait for a report. As Brady stalks up the trail, they slip into walkie-talkie lingo.

"Don't go far. Be ready to come back. Over."

After fifteen seconds, "Do you have a visual?"

"Negative on visual."

When he returns, they decide to split up, with Robbie heading around behind the barracks to attract attention while Nicco and Brady head up onto the ferny ridge above the outhouse. I sneak around to get a view of the enemy's goal where the defenders desultorily fend off mosquitoes and prowl for invaders. Robbie appears from near the old car chassis and immediately draws a couple of followers. Then, out of nowhere Brady zips in, pulling away the last defender, and Nicco makes a beeline for the goal, plunging in like sliding into second. Score. They both jump up in glee, yell, "Beautiful attack!" and then, much to my (and I think their) surprise, throw their arms around each other in a celebratory hug. It's a moment of pure joy.

The next day I talk to the boys about why they like the game. I try to get past the "fun" response and dig into the deeper learning. Brady comments,

> *Through the Whitehead Game, you get to know the island better. You learn all the little paths, how the swamps are connected. You have to listen and not do everything yourself. And you have to know when to stop arguing— to just accept that you've lost. You learn good sportsmanship.*

And with surprising insight, Robbie suggests,

> *I don't want to be stereotypical or anything, but lots of kids at this camp are really rich and will grow up to live in big houses with not much nature around and they'll pretty much do things by the book. So it's great to run around in the woods, follow paths, not follow roads, and find your own path to the destination. It's a really good lesson.*

Anne, the camp director, concurs about the deeper value:

> *I've been coming here for twenty years since when my father was camp director and Whitehead's crashing waves, salt spray, and beach rose are never far from my heart. I love this place and I think playing this game helps these boys to develop the same lifelong love of the Maine coast.*

At the end of their stay, the boys write in the journal. Echoes of the game resound on every page: "The Whitehead Game was awesome. It was scoreless after hours of sneaking and running in the woods, but it didn't matter." And my favorite, "Disney World is a flea compared to Whitehead."

JUST FUN AND GAMES?

So, that was fun, you might be thinking, but what's the point? Well, there are a lot of points. From a cultural preservation perspective, I think that the preservation of island games should be considered a part of the bigger picture of preserving island culture. Just as we want to preserve oral history, local landmarks, and endangered habitats, it's valuable to preserve the unique play traditions that adults and children shape together. I anticipate that the Whitehead Game has legs. In other words, it's a good enough game to be exported and used in other recreational settings where it will help to build healthy bodies in twelve ways, just the way new drugs from Amazonian flora can help cure cancer.

On another level I think these kinds of games create a love of place—first a love for the island where they emerged and then a broader love for natural places. Consider this. Remember Louise Chawla's study of the childhood experiences of environmentalists? Most environmentalists attributed their commitment to a combination of two sources, "many hours spent outdoors in a keenly remembered wild or semi-wild place in childhood or adolescence, and an adult who taught respect for nature." Lots of time rambling in neighborhood woods and fields and a parent or teacher who cared about nature were frequently cited as causal forces in the development of their own environmental ethics.

Mailboat skits aside, don't these island-play examples fit these guidelines? The island is the perfect "keenly remembered wild or semi-wild place" with clear boundaries that make exploring safe. And the presence of adults who teach respect for nature is present because in all of these examples, adults and children are cocreating these experiences. Adults provide the rules and parameters, adults often participate, and adults are there to help extract the deeper moral and ethical lessons.

Finally, island play binds families and communities together. In *Bowling Alone*, Harvard sociologist Robert Putnam (2000) explores the special conditions that create

vital communities. He was looking for sources of "social capital," which he defines as the predispostion of each individual to contribute to the quality of life in that community. Oddly enough, he found that villages with strong choral societies and soccer clubs had the greatest social capital. In these communities, there was a strong network of volunteerism, a disposition to help your neighbors, a greater willingness to serve on boards and committees, and as a result, a healthier, more vibrant community. In other words, playing and making music together helped to bind the community together.

In her essay "Lost Worlds: The Challenge of the Islands," Rachel Carson said,

> *Islands present a conservation problem that is absolutely unique, a fact that is not generally realized. This uniqueness stems from the nature of the island species, and from the delicately balanced relationships between island animals and plants and their environment…On these remote bits of earth, Nature has excelled in the creation of strange and wonderful forms.* (1949)

As we work to preserve island ecosystems and cultures, let's remember that the "strange and wonderful forms" of play are part of the glue that holds islands together.

CHAPTER 10
PLACE-BASED EDUCATION IN GUILFORD, VERMONT
Teaching Locally, Understanding Globally

by Matt Dubel and David Sobel

Prelude

The primary author for this essay is Matt Dubel, a graduate of the Department of Education's Integrated Learning Program at Antioch University New England in Keene, New Hampshire. A specialized concentration in this program trains elementary school teachers in place-based education. Place-based education is the process of using the local community and environment as a starting point to teach concepts in language arts, mathematics, social studies, science, and other subjects across the curriculum. Emphasizing hands-on, real-world learning experiences, this approach to education increases academic achievement, helps students develop stronger ties to their community, enhances students' appreciation for the natural world, and creates a heightened commitment to serving as active, contributing citizens.

In this essay, Matt describes his fall 2004 internship in Jennifer Kramer's sixth-grade classroom in Guilford, Vermont. The three major projects he describes have roots in the design principles. The Guilford Slate unit takes students on real Adventures to abandoned and operating slate quarries where they actually get to split slate—how exciting! In addition, there was a Hunting and Gathering component when the students gathered enough slate to make an elegant walkway in the school's entrance garden.

The Broad Brook project involved lots of Maps and Paths work—figuring out all the headwaters of Broad Brook and assembling how all the pieces of Broad Brook fit together. Then the integrating tour de force was the Small Worlds process of re-creating the brook in book form.

Finally, the Town Meeting simulation is an example of the maturation of the Fantasy and Imagination principle for middle school students. Teachers who conduct historical simulations or produce classroom plays understand the pedagogical virtue of creating classroom paracosms. And whereas becoming flower

ADVENTURE
◆

FANTASY & IMAGINATION
◆

MAPS & PATHS
◆

SMALL WORLDS
◆

HUNTING & GATHERING
◆

fairies is appropriate for young children, becoming adult townspeople addressing a fabricated, but possibly real, community problem is just right for young teens. John Dewey advocated that the classroom should be a laboratory for democracy, and that's clearly what's happening in Guilford.

IN A CORNER OF VERMONT

The sun's just breaking over Wantastiquet Mountain as I head south along the Connecticut River valley to Guilford, Vermont. It's the last day of school before winter break and, sadly, the last day of my internship. Turning off the highway to follow the twisting route that leads to Guilford Central School, my eye catches the outcropping of slate that abuts the exit ramp. After spending the past month investigating slate with the sixth-grade class, I see slate everywhere. It's part of the phenomenon that newfound knowledge actually enables you to see what was there all along. Think of learning to identify something—a white pine, a red-tailed hawk, an eastern swallowtail, anything—and then seeing it everywhere, like you've stumbled into some great abundance that can be accessed only by your ability to recognize it's there.

As I make the commute that I've driven each weekday for the past four months, it strikes me that this place that was so new to me in August is now familiar. Wallace Stegner writes, "No place is a place until things that have happened in it are remembered in history, ballads, yarns, legends, or monuments" (1993). What was once just another pretty Vermont landscape is now a place I see through the history of working with fifteen sixth graders and one exemplary teacher. As I drive through Guilford this morning, the sights out the window retrace the path of my internship. The white clapboard church ahead evokes the time we brought the students here to check out its magnificent nineteenth-century slate roof and to seek out the gravesite of a prominent quarry owner in its cemetery. This landscape abounds with our stories, the product of a season spent engaging students in learning language arts, social studies, science, and mathematics by using the raw materials of the community around them.

Guilford, Vermont, is a town of just over 2,000 people in the southeast corner of the state, just north of the Massachusetts border and just west of the Connecticut River. Don't picture the classic Vermont town green with a steepled church on one end. Instead, imagine several smaller villages, each little more than a crossroads today, although in the nineteenth century they were distinct communities with unique economies and demographics. Following Route 5, I enter into one of these—the village of Algiers—that lies just north of a string of slate quarries reputed to be the oldest in the nation. It was here, in these quarries, that our study of geology came alive this fall.

MINING SLATE

Walk into any school and the odds are good that you'll find a class studying geology. But so much of what passes as geology is bookishly abstract, mystifyingly disconnected from the earth beneath the students' feet. We decided to use the landscape of Guilford to illuminate our study of geology. And what a story we found: volcanism, ancient oceans, continental collision, intense glaciation, and a rock that vitally shaped the human history of this area. This intersection of the natural and cultural history of Guilford through the quarrying of slate became our hook, and a natural link that connected all the core curricula.

Accompanied by geologist John Warren, we ventured out to what was once the largest slate quarry in Guilford. After lots of talk about this metamorphic rock, it was a thrill to approach the old quarry and see the hills of scrap slate, then enter the quarry itself through the corridor cut into the rocky hillsides. On either side, the walls were sheer slate: some sheets vertical, some horizontal, some at odd angles. John explained how the metamorphism caused by continental collision over 200 million years ago might have caused the rock to form at such angles. Since the quarry walls extended at least forty feet above where we were standing, we tried to imagine how the slaters worked the quarry.

Before long, students were quarrying their own samples to take back to the classroom. Later, local quarry owner Pete Crossman took us out into his working slate quarry to show us how people really work with slate. After pointing out which veins were good for shingles, which were good for flagging, and which were without commercial value, Pete demonstrated how to split a big sheet and then let our students try. Wes and Kevin jumped in first, and with Mitch's help they managed to split a large slab, over three feet long. It was a triumphant moment.

Pete invited us to take that slab, along with as many as we could haul, back to school. Soon everyone was gathering slate and lugging slabs to the cars, from the burly boys who tried to lift them on their own to the enterprising team of girls who teamed up—sometimes three to a slab—to deliver them to the car. We gathered until the trunks of our cars sagged and we feared bottoming out on the dicey road out of the quarry. The plan was to use the slate to build a beautiful walkway through the school's entrance garden as a service learning project and a fitting testimony to the enduring significance of that rock to the town of Guilford.

Pete also showed us the fields where the shanties once stood that housed the slaters, mostly immigrants from Wales. So, back in the classroom we set out to learn more about the people who worked in the slate quarries. Students learned how to conduct research using census records and compiled lists of the actual Guilford residents who were slaters in 1860 and 1870. Since we were studying statistics at the time in mathematics, using the census records to create the profile of a typical slater became a perfect culminating project to develop students' data analysis skills. They tabulated data from the census reports, separated quantitative from categorical data, determined mean, median, mode, and range for quantitative data, and used their statistics to draw conclusions about the typical slater.

A grand story began to emerge, for us as well as for our students, stretching back over two hundred million years to the collision of continental plates and reaching right up to the present in the slate shingles that still cover the roofs of some of our students' homes. To help students pull together what they had learned and to assess their skills and understanding, we challenged them to create a PowerPoint slide show that would tell the story of Guilford slate to people in the school, the community, and beyond. Students broke into teams, each charged with gathering the words and images that would answer a key question:

How and when was the slate formed?

What are the characteristics of slate?

Where were the slate quarries and how did people quarry slate?

Who worked with the slate?

What was and is slate used for?

The process of sifting through all the accumulated information and identifying the salient points amounted to a massive exercise in summarizing and organizing. Seeing how the students distilled their experiences into the big ideas and supporting details convinced me that grounding learning in place isn't merely an effective strategy for teaching the content of natural or cultural history. It's also a valuable technique for helping students develop the thinking skills that make learning anything more efficient. Because the subject matter was local and relevant, it hooked the students, and they were eager to share what they knew with others. Because it was local, there was an interested community audience, and the awareness of this audience motivated the students even more. The students exercised their thinking skills; they wanted to do the job well, and summarizing and organizing information was essential to doing it. When students presented their work to a series of community audiences, the scope and quality of what they had achieved was apparent to all.

We hadn't set out purposely to construct a broad, interdisciplinary unit, but that's precisely what evolved as we pursued the interesting leads and intriguing questions in our study of slate. As a science exploration, we began to explore the basic geology, but the human connection to the rock was so pervasive that we were propelled into social studies. The social studies investigation yielded data that told the story quantitatively, so we launched into mathematics. And communicating what we discovered to a broader audience necessitated language arts. To leave out any one discipline would have weakened the academic rigor of the project and foreclosed that natural human curiosity to see where the story leads without regard to academic categories. Instead, our students saw the interaction between people and the land they inhabit in full spectrum. In the process, they honed inquiry and communication skills that cut across the boundaries of subject areas and disciplines.

FOLLOWING BROAD BROOK

Turning off of Route 5, away from the slate quarries, I pick up Guilford Center Road, which follows the contours of Broad Brook, one of the tributaries of the Connecticut River. Broad Brook's path, from its sources to its outlet at the Connecticut, takes place almost entirely in Guilford, making it a natural focus for our study of watersheds, streams, and rivers. Broad Brook flows along the edge of the woods next to the school, so one afternoon we led the students down to the banks of the brook, sat along its waters, and posed the question, Where does this brook start and where does it end? Our students are familiar with Broad Brook, since it flows past many of their homes and most everyone crosses it at least once on the way to school each day. But connecting that casual knowledge of the brook with a more systematic understanding of the movement of water was another thing altogether. Since we were just closing a geography unit, we challenged students to use topographical maps of Guilford to locate possible sources of the brook. From there, we mapped the various paths the tributaries take in forming the brook and the course the brook takes toward the Connecticut.

The big event was an expedition: a chance to follow the journey of Broad Brook from source to mouth. Starting in one of the places we had identified as a source, we journeyed along the brook's route by car, making periodic stops to observe the brook, take field notes, and make sketches (along with splashing a bit in its waters, of course). From steep and narrow to wide and lazy, the brook took on a life of its own. The students' task following the expedition was to tell the story of Broad Brook in the first person, from source to outlet, using their field notes and sketches as raw material. The stories were then illustrated with watercolors and made into accordion books. When unfolded, these books revealed a miniaturized version of the entire course of the brook. The project was conceived by a previous Antioch University New England intern, Betsy Carline, as an alternative to a prepackaged unit on rivers and streams. Having students transform their observations of a watershed into an illustrated story forges a brilliant connection between science, language arts, and visual arts. There's something about the way a river's course, with its beginning, middle, and end, tension and resolution, models the structure of a good narrative. And just as our geography study flowed seamlessly into the Broad Brook study, the intimate experience students gained of the erosive power of water made for a perfect segue into our study of geology.

If I continued driving on Guilford Center Road, eventually I'd climb to that meadow next to an old farm where we discovered Broad Brook emerging from a wetland. Instead, I turn onto School Road, not far from one of the old one-room schoolhouses. Until not that long ago, fourteen one-room schoolhouses served Guilford's children. I know this, and where they are, because Kristen and Elizabeth mapped the location of all of them. At the beginning of the year, we launched our geography study by having students create thematic maps of their town. Students chose an aspect of the town they'd like to map, and their choices are an indicator of what's prominent in Guilford and relevant to our students: bodies of water, sugar houses, farms, snowmobile trails, slate quarries, cemeteries, school bus routes, one-room schoolhouses, and students' homes. Using a combination of personal experience, fieldwork, and primary sources such as the official town history, students created a visual representation of one aspect of their place. Viewed together, the maps produce a remarkable portrait of a rural town. As Madison put it, "A lot of people think Guilford is this little dinky town, but you look at the maps and there's a lot here."

TOWN MEETING

Just before I reach Guilford Central School, I pass by the town office, an essential resource throughout the past months. Much of the primary source material—town maps, town ballots, town annual reports—that our students worked with came from the ever-helpful staff of the town of Guilford. Without those materials, today's big event wouldn't be possible. After studying civics and government for several months, today is the day of our Town Meeting simulation, in which students will deliberate on an issue as townspeople, using the same process that's used to make decisions in Guilford. In fact, Guilford Central School is the site of the annual Town Meeting, and to lend authenticity to our exercise we'll be using the Town Meeting gavel to call the meeting to order.

The gavel is a small detail, but it reminds us all of the connection between what we're doing and the real event that it simulates. The unifying premise throughout this fall has been to use Guilford as the reference point whenever possible to make learning more concrete and relevant. Walk into our classroom on any given day and you'd see piles of slate on the floor, local GIS maps lining the wall, charts of data copied from the 1860 Guilford census, or stacks of *The Official History of Guilford, VT*. We used authentic artifacts, such as the gavel from the Town Meeting; we visited pertinent locations, such as the slate quarries; and we consulted primary sources, such as the town report. We did this because the concrete details and local connections helped students make better sense of bigger concepts, whether the concepts at hand were mean/median/mode, plate tectonics, scale, first-person narrative, or democracy.

So our study of civics and government explored the two forms of democracy used in Guilford: representative and direct. We began during election season, and the authentic way to learn the process of representative democracy was to have the students do as citizens do. Our sixth graders can't vote, but they can do the next best thing: take a copy of the town ballot, a copy of the *Vermont Voter's Guide* with information on the candidates, make decisions on which candidates to support, and then lobby for their candidates with each other as well as the actual voters in the room. Interesting, real questions emerged that I suspect don't pop up when teachers use the ubiquitous, pre-packaged election materials with students: What is the Patriot Act? Should the government make sure everyone has health care? Do we have a responsibility to support our president during a time of war? What do the political parties stand for?

On Election Day, the seventh and eighth grades hosted a mock election, and while waiting in line to vote, the chatter among our students was about candidates: How many people were voting for Bush? Who was Wylie's pick for auditor of accounts? Who would the teachers vote for? The ballots for the mock election were simplified (all of the primary grades were participating as well) and the sixth graders came out wondering why Michael Badnarik wasn't on the ballot for president, or why the lieutenant governor's race was omitted. After you've worked with the real thing, the simplifications designed for kids seem, well, childlike.

To investigate direct democracy, we followed the same principle: have the students do what the adults do to run Guilford. So we started by examining the articles that Town Meeting considered that year, from the bold (Should the town call on the state to create a universal health insurance system?) to the commonplace (Should the town spend $55,000 on the volunteer fire department?). Then the students suggested articles that they'd like to consider in our own simulated Town Meeting. At last we arrived at a consensus: our town would decide whether to allow the development of a shopping mall in Guilford. The students chose roles, developed their points of view, and honed their arguments. Now this morning they will debate the article as townspeople, using the same procedure for decision-making that all towns in Vermont use.

With a bang of the gavel, I bring the Town Meeting to order and introduce the article. Thomas, as the developer of the project, wastes no time in moving the article and steps forward to make the case in favor. For the next forty-five minutes, students engage in a fascinating dialogue. Their comments touch on land use, environmental impact, trail access, community heritage, quality of life, economic development, the survival of small businesses, and the town budget. What I find remarkable is that many of their comments emerge extemporaneously and go beyond what they had prepared to say. Following proper dialogue procedure, they seem to listen respectfully to each other, then respond from the point of view of their character. I'm particularly touched by the way Kristen and Elizabeth speak persuasively on behalf of their characters' concern for the rural quality of Guilford. Kristen's character says, "There are so many busy places in the world, it makes Guilford unique and special and different."

It's wonderful to watch how students employ local knowledge gained in our studies this fall to analyze this particular scenario. Several students bring up their thematic maps to point out the location of the proposed development, and are able to speak with authority about the topography of the area. Just as the thematic maps enhanced our study of Broad Brook, which in turn enhanced our study of geology, this local knowledge came to bear on Town Meeting. Each project built on the others and added depth to the students' cumulative understanding.

Ultimately, the coalition of interests that support the shopping mall prevail, gaining a majority in a voice vote, and I adjourn the Town Meeting. Then an extraordinary thing happens. Without any prompting, the students get up and start to congratulate each other, allies and opponents alike. Witnessing this, I feel like I've flashed forward twenty years and am seeing these students after a real Town Meeting, acknowledging each other not as fictional characters but as fellow citizens, conducting themselves with civic dignity and mutual respect. Throughout these past months, we've sought to help our students come to know and care for their community at the same time that we've nurtured their intellectual growth, with the conviction that this local knowledge and care was the surest foundation for responsible citizenship. Watching these students today, I see it working.

CHAPTER 11
GLOBAL CLIMATE CHANGE
MEETS ECOPHOBIA

Prelude

Most educators realize we have to start doing something about global climate change in schools. But how is this issue most effectively integrated into an already jam-packed curriculum? And are there any developmental parameters that we should attend to in figuring out how and where climate change education should go? At all grade levels? Just in high school?

My desire is to approach these questions from a perspective that maximizes hope. If we lead with all the tragic implications of climate change, then we risk scaring children into despair. In Beyond Ecophobia *(1996) I suggested, "No [environmental] tragedies before fourth grade." Since global climate change certainly qualifies as an environmental tragedy, that guideline applies here. But, even in kindergarten, we begin to model living lightly in the classroom by such things as taking care of classroom plants and animals and turning off the lights when we leave a room. We create opportunities for children to practice ecological behaviors as part of the classroom and school culture.*

Essentially, I advocate for using the classroom as a microcosm of the school, the school as a microcosm of the community. By learning how to behave responsibly in the school, children are practicing the behaviors we want them to demonstrate as adults in the community. This mind-set is a manifestation of the Small Worlds design principle.

John Dewey (1916) advocated for considering the classroom as a laboratory for democracy; it's a small, controlled environment in which children can see all the operating pieces and understand how their behavior affects the whole system. Similarly, we should consciously conceptualize classrooms and schools as miniature ecological systems where children can shape positive outcomes—keeping the flower beds beautiful, reducing the amount of stuff thrown away, improving the air quality both inside the school and on the schoolyard. Seeing that their behavior makes things better in the small world of the school will give children hope that they can shape the big world as they grow.

Ever since Al Gore's *An Inconvenient Truth* brought global climate change firmly into the public consciousness and public schools, the cards, letters, and emails keep on coming. "Is it really appropriate for third graders to watch this movie?" worried parents and teachers ask me. Their deep concern: Is it useful, or counterproductively upsetting, for children to be educated about the world going to hell in a handbasket?

People ask me because in 1996 I wrote a little book called *Beyond Ecophobia*, advocating for honoring developmental appropriateness in environmental education. At that point, I railed against premature rain-forest education for young children. I was concerned about the curriculum message that *the rain forest is being destroyed and it's your responsibility, first graders, to save it!* This would have been like asking us children growing up in the early 1950s to find a cure for polio.

In a "My Turn" *Newsweek* essay, Brookfield Zoo educator and parent Kathleen Slivovsky framed the dilemma well by pointing out the problem with some eco-ardent children's literature—in this case, a book for preschoolers about extinct animals. Here's her portrait of reading this book as a bedtime story: "'L' is for Las Vegas Frog… People built the city of Las Vegas and paved over all the freshwater springs where this frog used to live. Sadly, we say good-bye to the Las Vegas frog"(Slivovsky 2005). The very last sentence of the book is, "Let's hope humans never become extinct."

"Night-night, Jimmy."

HURRICANES, OCEANS, AND ICE CAPS, OH MY!

The same thing is happening right now with global warming education. The ice caps are melting, mosquito populations are expanding and spreading serious diseases, hurricanes are getting windier, and we need children to understand that it's their responsibility to fix these problems. But no pressure!

Numerous media projects are in the works to address the current problem of global climate change and the solution, education for sustainability. There's a puppet-based television show aimed at four- to six-year-olds, another PBS animated program aimed at eight- to ten-year-olds, and child-sensitive versions of *An Inconvenient Truth*. I've recently been asked to be on three different advisory boards and to write the foreword for a new book on the science of global warming by noted children's book author and illustrator Lynne Cherry. Yikes! What do I say?

On the one hand, I believe that global climate change is caused by human behavior and we've got to do something about it fast. On the other hand, I'm concerned that prematurely recruiting children to solve this overwhelming problem will just make them feel helpless and hopeless rather than motivating them to walk to school instead of riding in their parents' cars.

I'm reminded of the Godzilla-meets-Rodan movies of my childhood. Godzilla is Global Climate Change and Rodan is Developmentally Sensitive Environmental Education. They're battling in the Tokyo of my mind and my convictions are getting trampled. So here's my attempt to conduct a bit of conflict resolution between the two.

THE HORNS OF THE DILEMMA

Parents and educators are of two very different minds when faced with this dilemma. After being trained as a global climate change educator by Al Gore and National Wildlife Federation educators, Lisa Shimizu, a programmer at the Seattle rock station KEXP, decided to create a child-friendly version of the *Inconvenient Truth* slide show. She simplified the content, mollified some of the tragedy, kept a reasonable amount of graphs and charts, and targeted it for use with eight- to ten-year-olds. After showing it to a large family audience with lots of elementary-aged children, an interesting Web dialogue ensued that framed the divergent points of view on the issue.

One parent, reflecting some of my concerns, said

One concern to at least be aware of is that if we hit kids (before sixth grade) too hard with environmental problems, they learn the facts, understand the issues are important, but don't become more environmentally active. Instead they may be overwhelmed. Younger kids may best be served by following the lead of Rachel Carson, and building a sense of wonder and love for the earth.

Responding to the above comment, another parent scoffed,

> *My son attended this show. He loved it and got a lot out of it. To those of you who worry about age-appropriateness, and unintended consequences, I say, "Oh come ON!" Obviously the critics haven't seen the show... In America we've grounded our kids with materialism, egoism, violence, killing, convenience at any cost...and you're worried about Ecophobia?*
>
> *Never mind that we are past the point of pussyfooting around. Our generation hasn't shown itself to have the gumption to fix our mess, so it falls upon our kids to actually do something. If we don't send children the message now while they're young, they'll grow up to be the greedy, consuming jerks we are.*

It's easy to see the virtue in both of these perspectives. Clearly both parents are after the same thing: figuring out the right way to educate children who will rise to the challenge of living ecologically responsible lives. Assuming that many of us agree on this point, let's look at what we know about creating learning settings that effectively cultivate ecological behavior.

KNOWLEDGE, ATTITUDES, AND BEHAVIOR

In the late 1990s I met with a prominent environmental funder in Boston to advocate for environmental and place-based education and to demonstrate how they help increase students' academic achievement. Impatiently, he responded, "Well, test scores are all fine and good, but what I really want to know is if these programs help kids become better stewards of the land and water. Does place-based education actually change their environmental behavior?"

Good question. And the answer to that has been changing over the past couple of decades. The conventional assumption in environmental education starting in the 1960s and 1970s was that knowledge leads to attitudes, which lead to behavior. In academic terms, Hungerford and Volk summarize, "If we make human beings more knowledgeable, they will, in turn, become more aware of the environment and its problems and, thus, be more motivated to act toward the enivironment in more responsible ways" (1990).

Let's look at how this might work. We teach kids that burning gasoline in cars produces carbon dioxide and that carbon dioxide causes global warming. As a result, they develop the attitude that limiting one's consumption of fossil fuels is a good and virtuous thing to do. Then, when it's time for them to buy a car (here's the behavior), they'll opt for the Prius over the similarly priced, flashier but fuel-guzzling Firebird.

Sounds good, but as Hungerford and Volk indicate, "Research into environmental behavior, unfortunately, does not bear out the validity of these linear models for changing behavior." Or, more simply, it ain't necessarily so. Just because children know that burning fuel creates carbon dioxide and that this is bad for the planet, they don't necessarily develop ecologically responsible buying patterns. Increased knowledge and a change in attitude don't necessarity translate into different behavior. It's more complicated than that.

One of the problems with this model is its assumption that knowledge precedes behavior. Schools have construed this to mean that it's the school's responsibility to provide the knowledge and maybe the attitudes now—the behavior will take care of itself in the future. So we assume that all this good learning will lead to good behavior later. This, in turn, means we are less likely to use schools to practice, in little ways, the behaviors we want children to develop in bigger ways later on.

It also turns out that the pathway to responsible environmental behavior is a bit trickier than knowledge leads to attitudes lead to behavior. It's more like a sense of agency and control leads to the knowledge of issues and action strategies, which lead to an intention to act, which under the right precipitating conditions, leads to environmental behavior.

One of the first things we need to help children learn is that their behavior makes a difference. Your feeding the kitty keeps the kitty healthy. Turning off the lights when you leave the room saves us money. This sense of personal responsibility leads to wanting to understand why turning off the lights saves money and why turning off the lights reduces carbon dioxide production. The sense of agency leads to a desire for knowledge and a desire to know other skills for reducing carbon dioxide production. This leads to the intention to make other changes, if and when the choices present themselves, which leads to responsible environmental behavior.

At the risk of gross oversimplification, what this suggests is that small behaviors lead to knowledge and attitudes, which lead to medium-sized behaviors, which lead eventually to bigger behaviors. But keep in mind that behaviors are possible only when choices present themselves. If the nearest Prius dealer is a hundred miles away, you're probably going to buy the Firebird. If you really believe in recycling but there's no convenient paper recycling system in your classroom, you're probably going to throw the paper away.

This is all a long-winded way of saying that we've been spending way too much time focusing on conveying environmental knowledge and way too little time on developing environmental behaviors. In addition, in most schools, we've got a situation of "Do as we say, not as we do." We disseminate knowledge about how environmental systems work but we don't design schools to be models of sustainable systems. And as we know, actions speak louder than words.

CATASTROPHE AND ECOPHOBIA

Then there's the issue of ecophobia—my contention that the overwhelmingness of environmental problems can breed a sense of ennui and helplessness. A fascinating study by the Swiss National Science Foundation (Finger 1993) looked at the relationship between different kinds of environmental knowledge and environmental behavior in Swiss adults. The study compared adults whose knowledge about the environment was based mostly on media presentations of ecological catastrophes versus adults whose knowledge about the environment came from extensive nature experiences and activism, mostly at the local level. Finger found that "Environmental behavior is less the result of learning and knowledge and more the result of particular environmental experiences," and that "Some environmental learning does not necessarily translate into more responsible behavior towards the environment and can even be counterproductive." In other words, too much knowledge about environmental tragedies actually discourages environmental behavior. Knowledge decreases behavior! If global warming is a done deal, why should I bother to do anything about it? If this is true for adults, who have well-developed capacities to shield themselves from information overload, think how this must be affecting children.

The author concludes his study with recommendations for environmental education programs.

First, "Nature experiences seem to be a necessary condition for any type of environmentally responsible behavior... In particular, nature experiences should be provided for the youngest generation."

Second, "Experiences of environmental activism emerge as another crucial condition for any environmental behavior... It is necessary that social and collective action be an integral part of any continuing education activity."

Third, "Fear and anxiety of environmental problems has the potential to turn environmental education into a counter-productive activity." Therefore, education about the problems should be substantially counterbalanced by opportunities to address the problem constructively.

Fourth, "When low fear is involved, environmental knowledge and information do make a difference in terms of environmental behavior."

Resonating with Finger's first suggestion is a 2006 Cornell study by Wells and Leckies that looked at the relationship between childhood experience and adult environmental behavior. They found that "Childhood participation in 'wild' nature, such as hiking or playing in the woods, camping, and hunting or fishing, is positively associated with environmental behaviors in adulthood." Rather than taking eight-year-olds to the global warming slide show, it might be more useful, in the long run, to take them fishing or blueberry picking.

What does this all mean for what we do on Monday regarding global climate change education with children? Let's bring together these guidelines with the previous discussion about the relationship between knowledge, a sense of agency, and environmental behavior.

SCHOOLS FOR CLIMATE PROTECTION

In light of the rapidly accelerating evidence of climate change, and the small window of opportunity in the next thirty years during which we might stabilize climate, the temptation is to jump to direct instruction. *Global warming is breathing down our necks so let's educate the kids to do something about it!* This is what motivated Lisa Shimizu to make her modified version of *An Inconvenient Truth*. And while this might be a virtuous endeavor, it's not the big answer. Instead, we have to take a deep breath and start to do the hard work of shaping classroom and school cultures that will grow stewardship behavior during the thirteen or so years of elementary through high school education. To do this we should honor the recommendations of the Swiss National Science Foundation.

The first thing we need to do is create comprehensive place-based education programs that connect children and curriculum to the nearby natural world. Keep in mind that much of the available research suggests a very strong link behind childhood nature experience and adult environmental behavior. Without that deep, abiding sense of comfort in and love for the natural world, no amount of chastising about turning off the lights or biking to school is going to make a bit of difference.

Next, we have to design schools as communities of care. Schools are used to this mind-set in regard to caring for people. The good work of the Northeast Foundation for Children, which trains teachers in the Responsive Classroom, is one example of shaping a positive classroom culture. The change here is that the ethic of care has to be extended to caring for the natural environment and eventually the global ecosystem. Just as teachers develop a set of classroom jobs where all children participate in the daily tasks that keep the classroom functioning, I recommend that schools develop incremental, progressive responsibilities for children at each grade level. These responsibilities would involve every teacher, student, and staff member in shaping a school environment that models environmental sustainability.

For example, some city and education leaders in Keene, New Hampshire, have started to explore the idea of "greening" the local school district. Cities for Climate Protection is a nationwide initiative, in line with the international Kyoto Protocols, to reduce greenhouse gas emissions. Over the past five years, Keene has emerged as an acknowledged leader among small New England cities. The conversion of much of the city's fleet to biodiesel, excellent recycling programs, the use of recaptured methane to generate power for the solid waste facility, and a willingness to redesign some of the road infrastructure to facilitate the reduction of car emissions are all illustrative of conscious local attempts to green the city.

The idea is to extend Keene's Cities for Climate Protection initiative with a parallel Schools for Climate Protection initiative. The goal would be to evolve the curriculum, staff development, and facilities management aspects of the schools so as to cultivate an ethic of stewardship in Keene students, reduce the greenhouse gas emissions of school operations, and provide models of low-impact lifestyles to the broader Keene community.

One core precept of this approach would be to create a developmentally appropriate, schoolwide model, a Ladder of Environmental Responsibility as shown in Table 11.1, which honors the learning dispositions and capabilities of students and teachers at the elementary, middle, and high school levels.

This ladder would provide a set of incrementally more challenging tasks for children throughout their school career. In traditional agrarian cultures, this ladder of responsibility is often seen in children's progressive responsibility for chickens in early childhood, goats in middle childhood, and a horse or cow in early adolescence. The knowledge required, the care-taking skills, and the size of the animal increase with the competence of the child. Similarly, one small independent school in St. Louis has a continuum of outdoor education challenges. In first grade, children do a simple overnight on the schoolyard, in fifth grade they relive Tom and Becky's night in a Missouri cave, by eighth grade they do a weeklong urban service week in a Southern city. What we're looking for is a set of stewardship responsibilities for each grade level in the school.

How would this work in K through 6 public school? The teachers and staff would divide the environmental care of the school into seven increasingly sophisticated rungs of environmental responsibility. Each grade level would be assigned to one of the rungs of the ladder. The tasks would involve some kind of daily or weekly attention. The Ladder would be devised in conjunction with the state-mandated curriculum.

Certainly, the science curriculum is one consideration, but all aspects of the language arts, math, and social studies curricula would be considered as well. For instance, garden maintenance responsibilities would be allocated to the grade level in which the Growing Plants science unit is taught. The sixth-grade language arts curriculum focus on persuasive letter writing would be connected to the letters home to parents about not idling their cars when parked in front of the school. A sample Ladder might look like the one in Table 11.1.

Going back to that Swiss National Science Foundation study, the second recommendation was that "Experiences of environmental activism emerge as another crucial condition for any environmental behavior... It is necessary that social and collective action be an integral part of any continuing education activity" (Finger 1993). My translation of this recommendation is that, in order to cultivate long-term environmental behavior, it's important to provide ongoing training in environmental activism. The best way to do that is by embedding children in a culture that gradually ups the ante of responsibility as children mature. Children are expected to identify problems, devise solutions, advocate for change, meet barriers, accept defeat, celebrate successes, keep trying. By working on small, manageable, cognitively accessible environmental problems at a microlevel, we'd be

developing the sense of agency, the locus of control that Hungerford and Volk identify as one of the crucial elements in shaping persistent stewardship behavior. It's this kind of cultural modeling that will provide the durable commitment to dealing with the more expansive, heavy problems of global warming at the community, regional, and national levels as children become adolescents and adults.

Table 11.1

	LADDER OF ENVIRONMENTAL RESPONSIBILITY	
	A model for elementary schools	
K	***Seasonal School Beautification***: Teachers and students responsible for weekly displays of flowers, rock gardens, winter twigs, and the natural displays that fit with seasonal celebrations of the solstices and equinoxes.	
1	***Flower Garden Maintenance:*** Teachers and students weed the gardens, put them to bed for the winter, start seedlings in the late winter, run the plant sale in early spring, bring the garden to life, install new plantings.	
2	***Schoolyard Vegetable Gardens:*** Teachers and students install raised beds, test and amend the soil, harvest vegetables, arrange for the harvest festival, put the garden to bed, put up the pickles, order the seeds in the spring, plant the garden, organize the volunteers for summer maintenance.	
3	***Maintaining the Schoolyard:*** Teachers and students keep the nature area or schoolyard clean, devise graffiti- and vandalism-prevention programs, help teach schoolyard games, work with school maintenance staff, create homes for wildlife, keep the bird feeders full, keep the running record of birds that visit the feeders.	
4	***Running the Recycling Program:*** Teachers and students design and run the paper-recycling program. They collect the paper and bring it to the collection site, and monitor classroom and school use in hopes of decreasing paper usage. Systems for other materials such as glass, aluminum cans, and inkjet printer cartridges are developed as the system matures.	
5	***Tending the Composting Program:*** Teachers and students work with school lunch staff to first design a pre-consumer composting program and eventually a post-consumer program. Fifth graders educate new students about what's compostable and what isn't. They also staff the post-lunch separation process. When the system matures, post-snack systems are developed as well.	
6	***Climate Change Team:*** Teachers and students are responsible for minimizing the carbon dioxide output of the school. They accomplish this with yearly projects to monitor and reduce electricity, heating fuel, and water consumption in the school. Students suggest changes in student/teacher/staff behavior to reduce consumption. Students and teachers work with building maintenance staff to use the healthiest cleaning products with the least emissions.	

Just a pipe dream? I don't think so. Pieces of this kind of approach have taken root in schools across the country. Schools are rethinking school lunch, creating biodiesel for school vehicles, initiating anti-idling campaigns, creating schoolyard wildlife habitats. The Ladder of Responsibility is an idea just waiting to happen. Be the first school in your community to create one and then let us know how it's working.

Epilogue
Ancient Greece in Vermont

It's Art Walk Night in Brattleboro, Vermont—first Friday of the month. All the art galleries are chock-full of browsers. It's hard to get a table at a restaurant; all the stores are open late. Down at the Latchis Theatre, there's an unusual place-based education project on display.

Sure, it's easy to teach local history, math, and ecology in the community, but what do you do when you have to teach ancient Greece? Well, it turns out that the downtown movie theater is the connection between life in rural Vermont and Zeus, Heres, Mt. Olympus, and even the scantily clad nymphs accompanying Dionysus. After Greek immigrant Demetrius Latchis's fruit cart burgeoned into a successful grocery business, he moved into the theater business. The Latchis Theatre, which was also attached to a hotel with an expansive ballroom, was one of fourteen theaters he built throughout New England. Respecting his homeland, the interior motif of the theaters is a tribute to ancient Greek culture. As you enter, you're met by an alabaster statue of Hebe. The vestibule ceiling is lined with reliefs and friezes of men and women enjoying themselves. The signs of the zodiac sprawl across the dome of the theater. Greek temples, replete with examples of Doric, Ionic, and Corinthian columns, fill the corners. Extravagant murals of the gods, goddesses, demigods, and titans line the walls.

It turns out that the theater director had been looking for someone to redo the antiquated, 1950s brochure interpreting the history of the theater and the significance of its Greco Deco interior decorations. Here was the perfect opportunity to engage students in content-rich Greek architecture and mythology and provide a real service to the community. Mrs. Kramer's seventh-grade class from Guilford took up the challenge. The class was divided into numerous working groups focused on different components of the theater. They had to take photographs, complete extensive research, and then create a well-crafted brochure to tell the story of the Latchis. Students had to write a grant application to get funding to pay for the printing

expenses. One of the students became the project manager and ran, with teacher support, all the planning meetings. Students had to deal with all those frustrating autoformatting hassles in Word as they fiddled with the graphic design of the pages. When you look at the final product, you think, "Seventh graders did this? It's so refined and classy!"

Were there any of the children and nature design principles at work here? Not really. There are numerous sources of good curriculum, and this project didn't really lend itself to being enhanced with the design principles in mind. But, of course, there's a twist to be shared.

Art Walk night provided the perfect venue for sharing their work with the community. After all, it's a perfect example of the kind of historical art culture that has shaped the character of Brattleboro. There was a flurry of activity the final week before the formal opening. Posters, with content extracted from the brochure, were created to enhance the student presentations. The Greek bowls and vases that students had also crafted had to be finished up. The brochure pages, fresh from the printer, had to be assembled. The emphasis was on getting everything just so—no typos in the posters, refinement in all aspects of the presentation.

As the students were planning the food and the final touches, a movement emerged. Many of them wanted to come dressed in Greek costumes, even become Greek gods and goddesses. Someone even wanted to come outfitted as a Greek column. Mrs. Kramer was hesitant. The whole idea was to demonstrate the sophistication of their learning and students' ability to do real work in the community. She didn't want the costuming to undercut the quality and seriousness of their work. One of the students responded, "Mrs. Kramer, the brochure and the posters prove that we know how to be serious. It's really good work. So it's OK for us to be a little silly." Good point, she thought, so she consented with trepidation.

And so you enter the lobby, get an erudite overview from the project manager, and then stroll into the vestibule and learn way more than you thought seventh graders could possibly know about the difference between bas-relief, raised relief, and engraving. Upon entering the theater you're met in succession by Athena, Cupid, and Poseidon, who interpret the architecture and murals. The togas, laurel wreaths, sandals, and staffs aren't silly at all. They embellish the whole effect. Of their own volition, the students had added a Fantasy element to the project. Their impulse to enhance the serious with the playful was just right, and it illustrated the students' personal immersion in the project.

Of course, there's a message here. The best curriculum serves as a bridge between the inner and outer worlds, between play and work, between dreams and reality. The best educational system will shape adults who both love the earth and are smart and competent.

REFERENCES

Almon, J., et al. 2000. *Fools' Gold: A Critical Look at Computers in Childhood.* The Alliance for Childhood. www.allianceforchildhood.net/projects/computers_reports.htm.

Apelman, M. 1975. "On Reading John Dewey Today." *Outlook: The Journal of the Mountain View Center* 17.

Ashton-Warner, S. 1963. *Teacher.* New York: Simon and Schuster.

Bigelow, B. 1996. "How My Schooling Taught Me Contempt for the Earth." *Rethinking Schools* 11 (1).

Brookfield Zoo. 2001. "The Hamill Family Play Zoo and Gardens." www.brookfieldzoo.org. Accessed December 2007.

Burroughs, J. 1919. "Nature Lore." In *Field and Study.* Boston: Houghton Mifflin.

Carson, R. 1949. "Lost Worlds: The Challenge of the Islands." *The Wood Thrush* 4 (5).

Chawla, L. 1988. "Children's Concern for the Natural Environment," *Children's Environment Quarterly* 5 (3): 13–20.

———. 1998. "Significant Life Experiences Revisited: A Review of Research on Sources of Environmental Sensitivity." *Journal of Environmental Education* 29 (3).

Cobb, E. 1959. "The Ecology of Imagination in Childhood." *Daedalus* 88 (3).

Cohen, D. and S. MacKeith. 1991. *The Development of Imagination: The Private Worlds of Childhood*. New York: Routledge.

Crossing, W. 1965. *Crossing's Guide to Dartmoor*. Dawlish, UK: David and Charles.

Dewey, J. 1916. *Democracy and Education: An Introduction to the Philosophy of Education*. New York: Macmillan.

Eastman, C. 1971. *Indian Boyhood*. New York: Dover.

Finger, M. 1993. "Does Environmental Learning Translate into More Responsible Behavior?" *Environmental Strategy: Newsletter of the IUCN Commission on Environmental Strategy and Planning* 5, February.

Fowles, J. 1966. *The Magus*. New York: Little, Brown.

Froebel, F. 1970. *The Education of Man*. Trans. W. N. Hailmann. New York: Augustus M. Kelley. (Orig. pub. 1885.)

Frost, R. 1916. "Birches." In *Mountain Interval*. New York: Henry Holt.

Glazer, S., ed. 2001. *Valley Quest I: 89 Treasure Hunts in Upper Valley Towns*. Vital Communities, White River Junction, VT.

Glazer, S., ed. 2004. *Valley Quest II: 75 More Treasure Hunts in the Upper Valley*. Vital Communities, White River Junction, VT.

Gleick, J. 1987. *Chaos: Making a New Science*. New York: Viking Press.

Gordon, K. and M. Brenes. 2005. *Cloud Forest School Spring Newsletter*, April. The Cloudforest School, Monteverde, Costa Rica.

Greenberg, J. 1977. "Engineered Education." *Outlook, The Journal of the Mountain View Center* 23.

Hawkins, D. 1973. " How to Plan for Spontaneity," In *The Open Classroom Reader*, ed. C. Silberman. New York: Random House.

Hoffman, E. 1992. *Visions of Innocence: Spiritual and Inspirational Experiences of Childhood.* Boston: Shambala.

Holling, Holling C. 1941. *Paddle-to-the-Sea.* Boston: Houghton Mifflin.

Hungerford, H. and T. Volk. 1990. "Changing Behavior Through Environmental Education." *Journal of Environmental Education* 21, no.3 (spring).

Jacobs, H. 2001. Unpublished lecture in author's collection, Keene, New Hampshire.

Kellert, S. 1985. "Attitudes Towards Animals: Age-related Development Among Children." *Journal of Environmental Education* 16 (3).

Levi, D. and S. Kocher 2000. "Virtual Nature: The Future Effects of Information Technology on Our Relationship to Nature." *Environment and Behavior.*

Levy, S. 1996. *Starting from Scratch: One Classroom Builds Its Own Curriculum.* Portsmouth, NH: Heinemann.

Louv, R. 1991. *Childhood's Future.* Boston: Houghton Mifflin.

———. 2005. *Last Child in the Woods: Saving Our Children from Nature-Deficit Disorder.* Chapel Hill, NC: Algonquin.

Maravall, D. 1991. Notes on a Problem Solving Activity in a Literature Study. Unpublished paper, Antioch University New England Graduate School, Keene, New Hampshire.

McGrath, C. 1997. "Pond Life," *Outside.* February.

McLerra A. 1991. *Roxaboxen.* New York: HarperCollins.

McSwigan, M. 1984. *Snow Treasure.* New York: Scholastic.

Millstone, D. 1989. "Adventures in Our Backyard Newsletter." Marion W. Cross School, Norwich, Vermont.

————.1995. *Elementary Odyssey: Teaching Ancient Civilization Through Story*. Portsmouth, NH: Heinemann.

Muir, J. 1913. *The Story of My Boyhood and Youth*. Boston: Houghton Mifflin.

Nagler, T. 2002. "Pine Island Camp: A Short History." In *Pine Island Camp, The First One Hundred Years*. Belgrade Lakes, ME: Pine Island Camp.

Nicholson, S. 1971. "How Not to Cheat Children: The Theory of Loose Parts." *Landscape Architecture* 62.

Nixon, W. 1997. "How Nature Shapes Childhood: Personality, Play and a Sense of Place," *The Amicus Journal* (summer).

Paull, D., and J. Paull. 1972. *Yesterday I Found*. Boulder, CO: The Mountain View Center for Environmental Education, University of Colorado.

Perrone, V. 1988. "What Should Schools Teach? Issues of Process and Content." *Insights into Open Education* 21 (4).

Peterson, B. 1993. "Animal Allies." *Orion* 2 (spring).

Powell, M. 2001. *Fort Culture: The Hidden Curriculum of Recess Play*. Cambridge, MA: School of Education, Lesley University.

Putnam, R. 2000. *Bowling Alone: The Collapse and Revival of American Community*. New York: Simon and Schuster.

Pyle, R. M. 1993. *The Thunder Tree: Lessons from an Urban Wildland*. Boston: Houghton Mifflin.

Robinson, E. 1977. *The Original Vision: A Study of the Religious Experience of Childhood*. London: Religious Experience Research Unit, Manchester College, Oxford University.

Rogers, L. 1996. *The California Freshwater Shrimp Project*. Berkeley, CA: Heyday Books.

Shepard, P. 1983. "The Ark of the Mind." *Parabola* 8 (2).

———. 1973. *The Tender Carnivore and the Sacred Game*. Athens, GA: University of Georgia Press.

Slivovsky, K. 2001. "Confessions of a Passionate Interpreter," Brookfield, IL: Chicago Zoological Society.

———. 2005. "My Turn: 'Save the Elephants—Don't Buy Ivory Soap.'" *Newsweek*, August 15.

Smith, M. S., J. O'Day, and D. K. Cohen. 1990. "National Curriculum: American Style," *American Educator* 14 (4).

Sobel, D. 1990. "Iguana Hunt." *Sierra*, November.

———. 1992. *Children's Special Places: Exploring the Role of Forts, Dens and Bushhouses in Middle Childhood*. Tucson, AZ: Zephyr Press (currently published by Wayne State University Press, reissued 2002).

——— 1996. *Beyond Ecophobia: Reclaiming the Heart in Nature Education*. Nature Literacy Monograph Series No. 1. Great Barrington, MA: The Orion Society.

———. 1998. *Mapmaking with Children: Sense of Place Education for the Elementary Years*. Portsmouth, NH: Heinemann.

——— 2004. *Place-Based Education: Connecting Classrooms and Communities*. Nature Literacy Monograph Series No. 4. Great Barrington, MA: The Orion Society.

Staff of Wild Olympic Salmon. 1996. Tracking the Dragon: An Environmental Game and Watershed Tour, Wild Olympic Salmon. Chimacum, Washington.

Stegner, W. 1993. *Where the Bluebird Sings to the Lemonade Springs*. New York: Penguin.

Strachota, B. 1996. *On Their Side: Helping Children Take Charge of Their Learning.* Greenfield, MA: Northeast Foundation for Children.

Thomas, D. 1940. *Portrait of the Artist as a Young Dog.* New York: New Directions.

Van Schagen, S. 2007. "Child's Play: Can Al Gore's Message Be Tailored for Kids?" *Grist: Environmental News and Commentary,* March 16. Available at www.grist.org.

Vermont Department of Education. 2000. Vermont's Framework of Standards and Learning Opportunities. Available online at http://education.vermont.gov/new/pdfdoc/pubs/framework.pdf.

Wells, N. M., and K. S. Lekies. 2006. "Nature and the Life Course: Pathways from Childhood Nature Experiences to Adult Environmentalism." *Children, Youth and Environments* 16 (1). Retrieved from www.colorado.edu/journal/cye/.

Whitehead, A. N. 1967. *The Aims of Education.* New York: The Free Press. (Orig. pub. 1913.)

Wilson, E. O. 1994. *The Naturalist.* Washington, DC: Island Press.

Wilson, F. 1999. *The Hand: How Its Uses Shapes the Brain, Language and Human Culture.* New York: Vintage.

Wordsworth, W. 1888. "Intimations of Immortality from Recollections of Early Childhood." *The Complete Poetical Works.* London: Macmillan. (Orig. pub. 1807.)

Index